FIGHTING CORPORATE ABUSE

Fighting Corporate Abuse

Beyond Predatory Capitalism

Corporate Reform Collective

PlutoPress
www.plutobooks.com

First published 2014 by Pluto Press
345 Archway Road, London N6 5AA

www.plutobooks.com

Copyright © Corporate Reform Collective 2014

The right of the individual contributors to be identified as the authors of this work has been
asserted by them in accordance with the Copyright, Designs and Patents Act 1988.

British Library Cataloguing in Publication Data
A catalogue record for this book is available from the British Library

ISBN 978 0 7453 3517 9 Hardback
ISBN 978 0 7453 3516 2 Paperback
ISBN 978 1 7837 1194 9 PDF eBook
ISBN 978 1 7837 1196 3 Kindle eBook
ISBN 978 1 7837 1195 6 EPUB eBook

Library of Congress Cataloging in Publication Data applied for

This book is printed on paper suitable for recycling and made from fully managed and
sustained forest sources. Logging, pulping and manufacturing processes are expected to
conform to the environmental standards of the country of origin.

10 9 8 7 6 5 4 3 2 1

Typeset by Curran Publishing Services
Text design by Melanie Patrick
Simultaneously printed digitally by CPI Antony Rowe, Chippenham, UK
and
Edwards Bros in the United States of America

Contents

Introduction

People are very angry about recent corporate abuses and about the way in which the capitalist system is operating. This is not just about one or two cases of unlawful or unethical conduct. It is about the nature of capitalism itself. The list of abuses that have emerged since the boom and bust over the last five years keeps growing:

- The level of tax avoidance by major international companies like Amazon and Google and many other household names is shocking. Some estimates put the total of corporate tax avoidance in the United Kingdom alone at some £12 billion a year, enough to plug almost one-tenth of the annual public sector deficit for 2012–13.
- The level of fat cat salaries for bankers and corporate executives just keeps growing more or less regardless of the performance of the companies they run. The latest figures for top salary increases stands at 14 per cent for 2013 while most ordinary employees have seen a real reduction in their take-home pay.
- The prices for gas and electricity and rail fares keeping rising well above inflation, and so do the dividends paid out by the utility companies to their international shareholders. The leveraged financing of these and other such companies is built on complex offshore corporate structures that are difficult to monitor or control.
- When things go wrong, as in all the major banks and with some railway franchises, it is the taxpayer who is expected to pick up the tab. 'Too big to fail' and 'essential services must be maintained' combine to protect the interests of private sector bosses and investors at public expense.
- And no one ever seems to be held accountable even when there is evidence of criminal, unlawful or grossly incompetent conduct by senior directors and executives. 'Fred the Shred' Goodwin is not the only senior banker who has walked away from the catastrophe he presided over with a massive pay out for failure.

It is no wonder that there is growing public anger at this kind of corporate capitalism The campaigns of activists in the Occupy Movement and in UK Uncut and other pressure groups have reflected a widespread public mood. Ed Miliband and others have struck a chord with the focus on 'predatory capitalism' and the need to curtail the dominance of major utility suppliers, the power of the multinationals and the dangerous and unproductive operations of international investment banks.

And yet corporate capitalism is essential to current economic systems throughout most of the world. It has produced generally better results in terms of economic activity and individual prosperity than most forms of state-controlled economic activity. Market forces and competition between different suppliers, producers and retailers have generally proved to be more efficient in the allocation of resources than strict state socialism, which has its own common forms of abuse and corruption. And the largest multinational corporations have undoubtedly introduced some much-needed forms of economic development in many developing economies, and have often paid higher salaries to their employees than more traditional businesses. But they have also exhibited and benefited from the standard practices of economic imperialism.

So there are no political or economic certainties in the choice of structures for business enterprise. The underlying concept of the corporation as the legal basis for large business enterprises is quite sound – the creation of a legal entity through which people or bodies with surplus resources can supply capital for investment in economic enterprises, the development of natural resources or the delivery of essential services. Company law provides the basic structures. But the providers of capital, whether they are private individuals or state bodies, have a good deal of freedom to determine the detailed structures for the management of the business by the directors and executives they have appointed, and can in return expect a fair share of the resulting operating returns or profits after the payment of wages and other costs of operating. If the business is unprofitable they must either provide more capital or lose what they have already contributed. Whether the model is state or private capitalism is less important than formal operating structure of a self-contained operating company or corporation which is expected to run the business or utility as efficiently as practicable.

It is this formal operating structure, usually contained in the memorandum and articles of association of a standard company, that is the key to an understanding of any corporate body. These are designed to deal with the obvious conflicts of interest between the investors, the managers and the employees within the company, not to mention the impact on external consumers and the public at large. In the standard model the investors or shareholders are granted the power to appoint and dismiss the directors, who in turn are granted formal control of the operation of the business. This normally gives the directors the power to decide on how to allocate the company's resources between the payment of dividends to shareholders and reinvestment in the business, how much to pay their employees and themselves, and most other major decisions on how the business or enterprise is run. But the standard model is not the only one. In co-operatives the memorandum and articles of association grant most of these major powers to the members or employees rather than the providers of capital, who are usually entitled only to a fixed rate of interest on their contributions. In state corporations the government, whether national or local, is usually given the power to give instructions to the directors on all major decisions, including how much of the available resources to pay to the national or local exchequer.

The obvious point is that there is a huge range of possible structures for corporate enterprises. So how did things go so wrong with the standard model, and how can they be put right? Some activists argue that it is the system of corporate capitalism itself that is the problem, and that the system must be smashed and replaced by something better, though precisely what and how we might get there is not usually explained or argued in any depth. 'Smash capitalism' is a great slogan but not a convincing policy option. A return to state control of all major economic activity is not on any realistic political agenda. And the record both of capitalism and of the more extreme forms of state socialism suggests that other more pragmatic reforms may be more effective and achievable.

A History of Success and Recurrent Scandal

The history of corporate capitalism shows that the system can work but that it is inherently open to manipulation and abuse. Since the invention of the modern form of financial capitalism in northern Italy and in the chartered trading companies in Britain and France, its progress has been regularly interrupted by scandals and crashes.

- The chartered companies, the Africa Company, the Hudson Bay Company and the East India Company in Britain, and their equivalents in France and Holland, which were formed in the 16th and 17th centuries and funded by the sale of shares, initially on a more or less private basis and later traded on the emerging stock exchanges, were a key element in initial exploitation and trade in the East and the Americas. But the public market in shares and the inflation of expectations soon led to bubbles and crashes – the Tulip bubble in Holland

and the South Sea Bubble in London – and to legislation to control unauthorised flotations, leaving it to parliaments and governments to authorise any new public trading companies.

- Statutorily authorised companies funded by the sale of shares built the canals and railways in Britain and elsewhere in the 18th and 19th centuries. But some were fraudulently promoted and failed in the crash of the Railway King in the 1850s.

- Open access to incorporation, as an alternative to parliamentary authorisation for chartered public utilities and the increasingly unwieldy private partnerships with large number of shareholding partners, was promoted by Gladstone in 1844. This was soon followed in 1856 by the grant of automatic limited liability for shareholders as a way of avoiding the interminable and costly litigation over shares in large private partnerships. Most manufacturing enterprises converted to corporate status in the latter part of the 19th century. But there were successive scandals over the accuracy of accounts and the solvency of some publicly traded companies, which led to increased legislative controls over auditing and disclosure.

- Two major legal developments in the late 19th century led to new problems. In Britain the controversial case of *Salomon* v. *Salomon* in 1896 led to the acceptance that anyone could set up a small private company with limited liability and paved the way for a massive expansion in the number of limited liability companies. This has facilitated the exploitation of creditors by unscrupulous small businesspeople and the proliferation of tax avoidance schemes based on the registration of complex webs of companies and trusts with no other purpose than the minimisation of tax by wealthy individuals. The battle to regulate tax avoidance of this kind is still unresolved.

- In the United States the major development was the acceptance that one company could own shares in another, leading to the development of large groups of company and monopolies in the oil, railroad and other major sectors. These were eventually broken up and controlled in the US Anti-Trust legislation of the 1930s.

- The post-war period saw the development of the major multinational corporations which expanded their operations into new areas both by taking over established companies and by the creation of new wholly owned subsidiaries. In some case they were required to establish joint ventures with newly independent governments in the developing world. Their increasingly complex formal legal structures and their tax arrangements are another of the unresolved issues of corporate regulation with which this book is concerned.

- The most recent significant development has been the growth of global hedge funds and sovereign wealth funds which have been able to assemble sufficient resources to purchase large or controlling stakes in major corporations on the international stock markets. They have also been able to influence the outcome of more commercial take-overs and mergers by what is called 'arbitrage' – the purchase of short-term stakes in target companies with a view to making trading profits on the market rather than engaging in any form of corporate governance.

All these developments illustrate the continuing battle between corporate directors and executives, their shareholders and market traders who seek to use and abuse the corporate economy for their personal financial advantage. They also highlight the need for action by governments to protect and develop their national economies by regulating and controlling abusive practices.

How This Book Can Point the Way to a More Acceptable Corporate World

The current range of these and other abuses is documented and explained in the chapters in Part I of this book. Chapter 1 considers the ways in which major companies can structure their operations to avoid or limit the taxes they pay to national governments. Chapter 2 describes the way in which auditors and accountants play their part in tax avoidance and covering up the true state of affairs in the companies they are paid to audit. Chapters 3 and 4 illustrate how the freedom enjoyed by major companies to structure themselves in complex corporate groups, both nationally and multinationally, allows them to evade liability for financial failures and ecological disasters and to avoid the impact of outdated regulatory systems. Chapters 5 and 6 illustrate how directors and executives are able to organise the affairs of their companies to promote their own financial interests and to take advantage of the fine-sounding but self-serving concept of corporate social responsibility to preserve a warped and self-interested view of the corporate economy. Chapter 7 explains how the operations of investments banks and market traders have contributed to the supplanting of useful productive activity by complex financial manipulation.

Part II of the book is about how those regulatory systems can be made more effective, not by relying on outdated received wisdom about depending on shareholders or non-executives to control executives or by exhortations for corporate social responsibility, but by developing more radical structural reforms of corporate governance, market trading and taxation. Chapter 8 sets out how the political economy of major corporations can be restated and reformed to achieve fairer corporate structures. Chapters 9 and 10 set out the ways in which the operations of major multinationals can be regulated and controlled, and how the international taxation system can be reformed to ensure that they pay a fair share of the taxes that are needed in all the jurisdictions in which they carry out their businesses. Chapter 11 shows how the structures for internal corporate governance can be reformed and developed to ensure a fairer distribution of decision-making power and a better way of promoting research and investment in productive manufacturing rather than socially unproductive financial services. Chapter 12 shows how the unproductive and disruptive activities of investment banks and market traders can be curtailed more effectively. Chapter 13 illustrates some of the ways in which smaller and more co-operative enterprises can develop and compete effectively with their larger competitors. Chapter 14 sets out how alternative structures for the control and management of large enterprises can be developed and facilitated by government action.

The key elements in this programme for serious corporate reform to outlaw and prevent the worst aspects of predatory capitalism and to develop structures to enable the benefits of more responsible corporate capitalism to be enjoyed by everyone, whether as shareholders, employees, consumers or the population at large, will be:

- rejection of the view that shareholder value must always prevail
- controlling the freedom of companies to use complex group structures to avoid taxation and other forms of legitimate regulation of their operations
- building new representative governance structures in which all interested stakeholders may play a positive role
- curtailing the self-interested and opaque operations of auditors and accountants
- curtailing the short-term interests and powers of markets and hedge funds
- promoting alternative forms of co-operative, participatory and not-for-profit forms of economic organisation for both public and private sector enterprises.

We shall continue to press for these reforms and hope that you will join us in our campaign for national and international action on all these issues.

The Corporate Reform Collective:
Tom Hadden, Paddy Ireland, Glenn Morgan, Martin Parker, Gordon Pearson, Sol Picciotto, Prem Sikka and Hugh Willmott

Part I

The Abuses

1

Tax Evasion and Avoidance

Modern corporations are not independent of the state, but intricately connected with it in many ways. Yet our political leaders generally behave subserviently to businesses bosses, so that corporate power dominates political power. Much of this results from manipulation of the corporate form itself. Nowhere is this seen more clearly than in relation to taxation.

The revenues lost through tax avoidance, including those relating to corporate practices, are hard to estimate, but the European Union claims 'the level of tax evasion and avoidance in Europe to be around €1 trillion [£830 billion or US$1.25 trillion]',[1] equivalent to 7–8 per cent of the gross domestic product (GDP) of all EU member states. The US Treasury has estimated its tax gap (tax avoidance, evasion and arrears) to be $385 billion.[2] A large number of corporations, including Amazon, Apple, eBay, Facebook, Google, Microsoft and Starbucks, have been on the radar of parliamentary committees for avoiding taxes through complex organisational structures.[3] The amounts are a stark reminder of how tax avoidance forms an integral part of corporate profitability.

It is sometimes argued that companies should not be taxed at all, since taxes are a cost which they pass on to their customers. This rests on the mistaken view that a company is no more than a bundle of contracts. In reality, a company is a form of property protected by the state. The privilege – it should not be regarded as a right – of incorporation gives shareholders the protection of limited liability, justified by the advantages of enabling the combination of factors of production for large-scale economic activities. This protection enables companies to reap super-profits from economies of scale and scope, and to accumulate large concentrations of capital. Unless their profits are taxed, they will grow even bigger, further distorting competition. Furthermore, if companies were not taxed, the corporate form could easily be used to shelter all kinds of income from taxation.

Behind a wall of secrecy corporations are able to devise complex schemes to boost their profits and meet incessant stock market pressures to report higher profits. Tax avoidance also personally benefits business executives because their remuneration and status is often related to reported profits. In these tasks, corporations are advised and guided by an established tax avoidance industry fronted by accountancy firms, lawyers and financial services experts.[4] The system sustains a vast army of professionals engaged in both avoidance and evasion not only of tax but also banking and financial and other forms of regulation, resulting in enormously wasteful expenditures for both firms and governments.

In a globalised world, the distinctions between domestic and global are blurred, and almost all big companies are able to play the tax avoidance games. A few examples will help to illustrate the issues

Corporate Tax Trickery

Within major corporations, the taxation department/division often acts as a profit centre. It is assigned profit and revenue generation targets, and the promotion and the salary increments of its members often depend on meeting the targets. The promotion of tax avoidance schemes by a highly profitable division within Barclays Bank is a telling example, which unusually led to a public rebuke from the government. This rebuke might have curbed two tax avoidance schemes but does not deal with the corporate love affair for tax avoidance or tax havens. A 2013 report published by Action-Aid, summarised in Box 1.1, chastised Barclays for promoting investment in Africa through tax havens, all with the aim of increasing corporate profits and depriving millions of people of much-needed education, healthcare and social infrastructure.[5]

It is not just financial institutions: other corporations can also arrange their financial affairs in ways that avoid taxes. Companies can use their ownership structures to effectively shift profits and avoid taxes. A good example of this, as shown in Box 1.2, is the strategy adopted by a US private equity firm to enable it to capture and relocate the finances of Boots the Chemists, a major pharmacy chain in the United Kingdom, and to save around £1 billion in tax.

Corporate tax avoidance is not just a problem in the United Kingdom, but an issue wherever the corporate form has taken hold. US companies like Enron and WorldCom used offshore havens and artificial royalty programmes and management fees to reduce taxable profits.[6] The Chinese government claims that 'Tax evasion through transfer pricing accounts for 60 percent of total tax evasion by multinational companies'.[7] A Chinese government official added that 'almost 90 per cent of the foreign enterprises are making money under the table. ... most commonly, they use transfer pricing to dodge tax payments'.[8] A former senior fellow of the

---

Box 1.1 Tax avoidance promotion by Barclays Bank

Barclays Bank, a UK-based major international financial institution, came under public scrutiny because of the mismatch between its profits and taxes. For the years 2010–12, Barclays reported pre-tax profits of £5.7 billion, £3.2 billion and £4.8 billion respectively, but paid UK corporation tax of £147 million in 2010, £296 million in 2011 and £82 million in 2012.[9] One of the reasons for the mismatch between profits and tax is the existence of its tax division, which generated revenues of more than £1 billion a year between 2007 and 2010. One of its roles was to craft tax avoidance schemes. In 2012, the UK government took the rather unusual step of blocking two tax avoidance schemes which could have enabled Barclays and/ or its clients to avoid around £500 million of UK corporate tax.[10] A Treasury press release referred to both schemes as 'highly abusive' and 'designed to work around legislation that has been introduced in the past to block similar attempts at tax avoidance'.[11] The first scheme was designed to ensure that the commercial profit arising to the bank from a buyback of its own debt would escape corporation tax. The second scheme involved the use of authorised investment funds (AIFs), and sought to convert non-taxable income into an amount carrying a repayable tax credit in an attempt to secure 'repayment' from the Exchequer of tax that has not been paid.

Brookings Institution has argued that transfer pricing is used by virtually every multinational corporation to shift profits at will around the globe.[12] So in the next section we look at the root cause of the ease with which companies are able to shift profits and avoid taxes.

International tax avoidance by multinational or transnational corporations (TNCs)[13] exploits the tax haven and 'offshore' secrecy system, which was originally devised by and for them. However, tax havens are now also used for all kinds of evasion, not only of taxes, but of other laws, facilitating money-laundering for public and private corruption, terrorism, and other criminal activities. The offshore system has particularly distorted the finance sector, as an element in shadow banking and other techniques which contributed to the excessive leverage, helping to feed the bubble which caused the financial crash of 2007–09.

Box 1.2 The takeover and detaxing of Boots the Chemists

Boots was set up in Nottingham in the United Kingdom in 1849, and in July 2006, after a merger with Alliance Unichem plc, it became known as Alliance Boots. In 2007, the merged entity became the subject of the largest-ever leveraged buyout, led by the US private equity firm Kohlberg Kravis Roberts & Co. LP (KKR). KKR acquired Alliance Boots for about £12 billion through its holding company in Gibraltar. The company continued to trade in the United Kingdom with the same brand name but was reincorporated in the low-tax canton of Zug in Switzerland. KKR holds its stake in Alliance Boots through various funds and finance companies located in the Cayman Islands and Luxembourg.

The acquisition was funded by a debt of £9 billion, and most of it has been left on the balance sheet of the UK operations. This potentially enables the company to write off the interest payments against profits even though profitable activities are carried out in other places, often low-tax jurisdictions. Alliance Boots operates in 25 countries and has an annual turnover of £22 billion. It has virtually no revenues in Zug and about 68 per cent of its trading profits come from the United Kingdom. The leveraged buyout and the loading of debt to the United Kingdom enabled the company to virtually eliminate its corporate tax liability in the United Kingdom in 2008. A report published by War on Want and UNITE states that the uneven allocation of the debt and the resulting tax relief on interest payments has enabled Alliance Boots to reduce its taxable income by some £4.2 billion for the six years to 2013. This has reduced the company's UK tax bill by between £1.12 to £1.28 billion.[14]

Outdated Principles in International Tax Law

These problems result from a deep structural flaw in the international tax system. This flaw is the failure to treat multinationals according to the economic reality that they operate as integrated firms under central direction.[15] Instead, a principle has become gradually entrenched that they should be taxed as if they were separate enterprises in each country dealing independently with each other. This can be referred to as the Separate Enterprise – Arm's Length Principle (SE-ALP). For example, FTSE100 companies have 34,216 subsidiary companies, joint ventures and associates, including 8,492 in tax havens that levy little or no tax on corporate profits.[16] Under the current practices, they are all treated as separate taxable entities even though they have common shareholders, boards of directors, strategy, logos and websites. This not only allows but encourages multinationals to organise their affairs by forming entities in suitable jurisdictions to reduce their overall effective tax rate by a variety of means.

Companies say that they only obey the rules decided by governments. But this is disingenuous. Business advisers and lobbyists are also heavily involved in designing the rules. Perhaps even more importantly, they are also central to moulding how the system works in practice, through the mutual understandings of business representatives and regulators. These technical specialists form a closed community of interpretation, reinforced by the movement of individuals from government service to working as business advisers – and less often in the other direction.

International tax treaty provisions are still based on models drawn up under the League of Nations in 1928, when international investment consisted mainly of loans.[17] The treaty models gave the state of residence of the investor the primary right to tax the income from investment (interest, dividends, fees and royalties), while the host country where the business was located could tax its profits. Some multinationals had emerged by the 1920s, and the rules were adapted for them, by requiring branches and affiliates in different countries to be treated as if they were independent entities dealing at arm's length. However, to prevent 'diversion' of profits, the treaty models provided that tax authorities could adjust their accounts, and national laws gave them powers generally to ensure that the levels of profit of branches or subsidiaries of foreign firms were similar to those of local competitors, or a fair reflection of their contribution to the firm as a whole.

Locating Offshore and Profit Shifting

The multinationals that developed in the last half-century are very different. As business organisations they are highly integrated and centrally directed, but in legal form they consist of often hundreds of different affiliates. In the past few decades tax-driven corporate restructuring has mushroomed, using complex structures designed to take advantage of national tax rules, especially regarding where a company is considered to be resident, and where the sources of its income are. In simplified terms, three stages and types of structure can be identified.

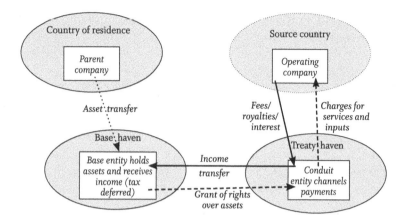

Figure 1.1 Basic tax avoidance strategies

First, and most basic, is a 'stepping stone' arrangement (see Figure 1.1). An operating affiliate in a source country can make payments of fees for services such as headquarters management, royalties for intellectual property rights (IPR), and interest on loans, all of which are allowed to be deducted to reduce its taxable business profits. These payments flow to one or more affiliated holding companies, in a country with suitable tax treaties, such as the Netherlands, Switzerland or Singapore, so they will be subject to no or low withholding taxes. The bulk of the income is passed through this conduit, leaving it with a nominal level of profit, to a 'base' affiliate in a classical tax haven, such as Bermuda or the Cayman Islands, which does not tax such profits. This ensures low effective tax rates for the firm's foreign earnings, if they do not need to be repatriated to finance dividends to shareholders. They can be retained for reinvestment by making loans to the firm's affiliates, even to the parent, which also means that the interest can be deducted from income.

This ability to finance expansion through lightly taxed retained earnings has long been a major competitive advantage for multinationals. Next, they began to reorganise their operations to exploit tax advantages offered by states. In the 1990s, competition to attract inward investment led many countries to provide tax holidays, which were attractive especially for mobile businesses.[18] For example, computer chip manufacturer Intel opened major manufacturing facilities in Puerto Rico, Malaysia, the Philippines, Ireland and Israel, all of which offered tax holidays.[19] This type of avoidance was harder to combat than the basic 'stepping stone' arrangement, because these affiliates were not mere letter-box companies receiving only 'passive income', which is a key criterion in national laws on 'controlled foreign corporations' (CFCs) enacted by the United States and a number of other countries to combat tax avoidance. It is difficult to treat such an affiliate as a CFC so as to make its income directly taxable as attributable to its parent because it is engaged in active business.[20] Multinationals have, of course, also lobbied to limit the scope of the passive business definitions, so that many financial services activities have been excluded. Consequently, the profits of hedge funds and private equity firms can be treated as arising in zero-tax countries, such as the Cayman Islands, simply because their transactions are booked by an affiliate there, even though the investment decisions are made and trading conducted in major financial centres, such as New York and London.

Building further on this strategy, corporations began to reorganise their legal structures by splitting various functions and assigning them to affiliates which were organised or located to minimise tax. This became much easier with the shift to the digital economy, which greatly facilitated international communication, enabling firms both to manage their own international value chains, and to deal with customers anywhere in the world. For example, sales to customers can typically be booked to one affiliate, while others deal with activities such as marketing, customer support, delivery and logistics. The main profit flow of course is attributed to the sales affiliate, located in a suitable jurisdiction where such income can be low-taxed, while the other affiliates are characterised as contractors, making relatively low profits on the specific operations for which they are supposedly responsible. For example, Amazon in Europe separates the functions of sales and website operation (attributed to Amazon SARL Luxembourg) from customer support, warehousing and order fulfilment, which are done in each country close to its customers. Similarly, Google books its sales of advertising to an affiliate in Ireland, with the income then flowing to another company formed in Ireland but considered to be resident in Bermuda (see Figure 1.2).[21]

These are some of the tax avoidance strategies used to create untaxed 'stateless income',[22] contributing a large slice of the billions of lost government revenues discussed at the start of this chapter. As can be readily understood from this brief analysis, it is the inappropriate nature of the concept of SE-ALP at the heart of the international tax system that provides the perverse incentives for multinationals to devise these elaborate corporate structures.

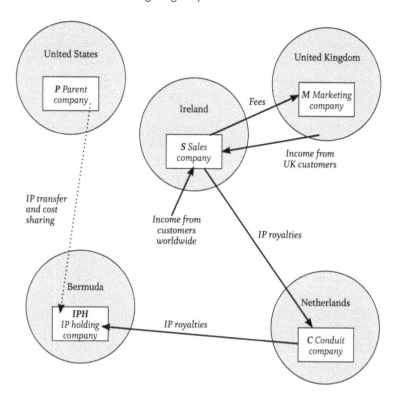

Figure 1.2 The double-Irish Dutch sandwich

The US parent (P) transfers rights to intellectual property (IP) to a company formed in Ireland but controlled from and therefore treated under Irish law as resident in Bermuda (IPH). IPH has a cost-contribution contract with P to help finance further development of the IP from its income, to justify the original sale of the IP under US transfer pricing rules. Another company (S) both formed and controlled in Ireland receives large income flows from operating the worldwide business (e.g. selling advertising). However, the net profits of S are low, because it pays large royalties for the IP rights. These are channelled through a conduit company C in the Netherlands (so that no withholding taxes are paid to Ireland), which deducts a small handling charge and pays the bulk of the IP royalty income to IPH in Bermuda. Although customers in countries such as the United Kingdom deal with another local affiliate company M, it is treated as providing only marketing or other customer support services. The actual sales contracts are concluded with the Irish sales company, which pays the M a fee for the marketing services.

What Can Be Done About It

These abuses cannot be dealt with effectively under the current principles of international tax law. What is needed is a radical overhaul of the system. This is at last coming to be recognised at both national and international levels. The Organisation for Economic Co-operation and Development (OECD) and the G20 group of leading economies have both embarked on a serious consideration of the issues, as shown in the concluding report of the G20 meeting in Fermanagh in 2013. The essential elements in any effective reform of the system are:

- the adoption of the principle of unitary taxation under which taxable income or profits are allocated to individual tax jurisdictions on the basis of real business activity
- effective international tax coordination to ensure that multinational corporations cannot play one country off against others by claiming or negotiating special tax advantages.

The way in which this new system can best be developed and implemented will be discussed in detail in Chapter 10.

2

Cover-Up Accounting and Auditing

A UK government investigation into corporate frauds in 1997 concluded that too many executives at major corporations have a 'cynical disregard of laws and regulations ... cavalier misuse of company monies ... contempt for truth and common honesty. All these in a part of the City [of London] which was thought respectable'.[1] Still, the 'greed is good' culture remained the centrepiece of political wisdom. Peter Mandelson, UK Secretary of State for Trade and Industry during 1998 and 2008–10, said that the government was 'intensely relaxed about people getting filthy rich'.[2]

The destructive effects of this neoliberal culture were highlighted in the financial crash of 2007–09. Countrywide, once the largest US subprime mortgage company, was found guilty of fraud.[3] The Lloyds Banking Group was fined £28 million for promoting a culture of mis-selling financial products.[4] Barclays, Deutsche Bank, Royal Bank of Scotland (RBS), Société Générale, UBS, JP Morgan and Citigroup were fined €1.71 billion for participating in illegal cartels to fix the London interbank offered rate (LIBOR) and the Euro Interbank Offered Rate (EURIBOR).[5] HSBC was fined $1.9 billion for having poor internal controls and facilitating money laundering by terrorists and drug kingpins.[6] Standard Chartered paid a fine of over $300 million for money laundering and sanction busting.[7] All of these banks boasted non-executive directors, audit and ethics committees, but none provided information about any of the above practices.

The Silence of the Auditors

In common with most other banks, all these financial institutions were audited by PricewaterhouseCoopers, KPMG, Deloitte & Touche and Ernst & Young, collectively known as the 'Big Four' accounting firms, whose combined annual worldwide income is around US$115 billion. They audit 99 per cent of FTSE100 and 96 per cent of FTSE250 companies, and dominate the global auditing market. But none of them said anything about the anti-social practices which formed the basis of bank profits. Indeed, New York regulators fined Deloitte $10 million and banned it from financial sector consultancy work for one year for 'misconduct, violations of law, and lack of autonomy during its consulting work at Standard Chartered on anti-money laundering issues'.[8]

Auditors are the private police force of capitalism, supposedly independent of company directors. They have more powers than the police, and without any court order can demand any information and interview any person to understand the financial position of the audited entity. Nominally, company auditors are appointed by shareholders, but in reality they are dependent on directors for their appointment and the resulting fees. They can remain in office for decades and thus build a fee dependency and collusive relationship with directors. Auditors are permitted to sell a wide range of consultancy services, including tax avoidance, to their audit clients. They audit the very transactions that they themselves have created. Appeasement of company directors is a key requirement as no one wants to lose a client that can provide huge fees for decades. For example, the late British tycoon Robert Maxwell plundered his employees' pension fund, but auditors Coopers & Lybrand (now part of PricewaterhouseCoopers) continued to give his business empire a clean bill of health even though parts of that empire did not keep proper accounting records. A UK government investigation noted that audit staff were instructed by the senior partner that the 'first requirement is to continue to be at the beck and call of RM [Robert Maxwell], his sons and staff, appear when wanted and provide whatever is required'.[9]

The audit contract, working papers, audit evidence, correspondence between auditors and directors, details of the composition of audit teams or the time spent on the job are not publicly available. Regulators, such as the UK's Financial Reporting Council (FRC) and the US Public Company Accounting Oversight Board (PCAOB), do get access to some of the auditor files to check the quality of work. But in auditing circles quality means checking compliance with auditing standards issued by the regulators rather than interfering with the entrepreneurial culture that prioritises self-interest. These standards are not formulated by parliament but by regulatory bodies dominated by the auditing industry, and are often the lowest common denominator.[10] The standards do not require auditors to detect or report fraud,[11] warn anyone about impending bankruptcy, or comment on the efficiency and effectiveness of corporate practices.

In the case of *Man Nutzfahrzeuge AG & anor v. Freightliner Ltd & anor*[12] the accounting firm admitted that it had been negligent in auditing the accounts, but escaped any liability because under the UK Companies Act 2006 auditors do not owe a 'duty of care' to any individual shareholder, creditor, employee, pension scheme member or any other stakeholder affected by auditor negligence. Rather the duty, in general, is to the company, and if by hook or crook a fraud-ridden company survives, auditors escape all repercussions.[13]

The absence of effective regulation and public accountability, and self-interest are the key ingredients of audit failures. No lessons were learned from the auditor complicity in the United Kingdom's mid-1970s banking crash, the US Savings & Loan crisis of the 1990s,[14] or the 1995 collapse of Barings Bank.[15] A US Senate report on the 1991 closure of Bank of Credit and Commerce International (BCCI), the biggest banking fraud of the 20th century, said that auditors had 'become BCCI's partners, not in crime, but in cover up'.[16] In 2001 the fraud-infested US energy giant Enron collapsed. Its auditors, Arthur Andersen, had always given the company a clean bill of health, and collected $25 million in audit fees and $27 million in consultancy fees in the final year of the company's life. A similar pattern was repeated in 2002 at WorldCom, where Andersen collected $47.1 million in auditing and consultancy fees between 1999 and 2001, and the company received the customary clean bill of health.[17]

The pattern of auditor silence was repeated in the 2007–09 banking crash. Prior to the crash, banks published healthy profits and their executives collected performance-related remuneration, but all was not what it seemed. Some small banks began to crash in early 2007. By September 2007 anxious savers were forming queues outside the branches of the UK Northern Rock to retrieve their savings. By October 2008, the Royal Bank of Scotland was teetering and the chancellor of the Exchequer said that the country was just two hours away from financial meltdown.[18] There were no clues in the opaque audited accounts published by banks. They all complied with the international financial reporting standards (IFRSs) issued by the International Accounting Standards Board (IASB),[19] but some $5,000 billion of assets and liabilities were not reported in their balance sheets.[20] Some banks showed assets, especially subprime mortgages, at highly inflated values. Derivatives have long been a 'powerful tool for inflating company profits by hiding losses and hence the risks of company operations'.[21] The chief executive of a leading

---

Box 2.1 *Balance sheet manipulation by sale and repurchase of assets at Lehman Brothers*

Lehman Brothers used an accounting gimmick codenamed Repo 105. Under this $50 billion scheme Lehman sold assets just before its financial year-end for around 5 per cent less than the balance sheet value, with an agreement to buy them back shortly into the next accounting period for the amount of sale plus interest. The resulting cash was used immediately to pay debt and thus show lower liabilities and an improved leverage ratio. The insolvency examiner said that 'the only purpose or motive for the transactions was reduction in balance sheet ... there was no substance to the transactions'.[22] The bank's auditors Ernst & Young (E&Y) collected $31 million in fees in 2007 and knew that Repo 105 had been used for several years by Lehman. The insolvency examiner concluded that 'the firm's outside auditor, was professionally negligent'.[23] A subsequent writ by the New York attorney general alleged that 'E&Y substantially assisted Lehman Brothers Holdings Inc ... now bankrupt, to engage in a massive accounting fraud, involving the surreptitious removal of tens of billions of dollars of securities from Lehman's balance sheet in order to create a false impression of Lehman's liquidity, thereby defrauding the investing public'.[24]

---

financial advisory business argued that a 'big part of the problem is that accounting rules have allowed banks to inflate the value of their assets; accounting has become a new exercise in creative fiction, with the result that banks are carrying a lot of "sludge" assets clogging up the balance sheet.'[25] Banks were estimated to have some $1.2 trillion of bad debts and toxic assets on their books.[26]

Banks were overleveraged and had little capacity to withstand any shocks, but auditors kept quiet. Bear Stearns had a gross leverage ratio (the ratio between total assets and shareholder funds) of approximately 33:1 prior to its collapse. Lehman Brothers, the fourth largest investment bank, had a leverage of more than 30:1. With this leverage, a 3.3 per cent drop in the value of assets would wipe out the entire value of equity and make the bank insolvent. However, almost all distressed Western banks received their customary clean bill of health from their auditors.[27] Some went bust within days of receiving endorsement from their auditors. For

---

Box 2.2 *Specialist advice ignored by the audit team at New Century Finance Corporation*

New Century Financial Corporation, the second largest originator of subprime residential mortgage loans in the United States, was an early casualty of the banking crash in 2007. Its insolvency examiner reported:

> *KPMG's [audit] engagement team acquiesced in New Century's departures from prescribed accounting methodologies and often resisted or ignored valid recommendations from specialists within KPMG. At times, the engagement team acted more as advocates for New Century, even when its practices were questioned by KPMG specialists who had greater knowledge of relevant accounting guidelines and industry practice. When one KPMG specialist persisted in objecting to a particular accounting practice ... an objection that was well founded and later led to a change in the Company's practice, the lead KPMG engagement partner told him in an email: 'I am very disappointed we are still discussing this. As far as I am concerned we are done. The client thinks we are done. All we are going to do is piss everybody off.'[28]*

---

example, Lehman Brothers received an unqualified audit opinion on its quarterly accounts in July 2008 from Ernst & Young, but filed for bankruptcy in September 2008. Bear Stearns received an unqualified audit opinion on its accounts in January 2008 from Deloitte & Touche and was rescued in March 2008. Carlyle Capital Corporation received an unqualified audit opinion from PricewaterhouseCoopers on 27 February 2008 and was placed in liquidation on 12 March 2008.

The banking crash once again revealed the cosy relationship between auditors and their paymasters. The treatments of some highly suspect financial transactions in Lehman Brothers and New Century Finance Corporation provide striking illustrations, as shown in Boxes 2.1 and 2.2.

Auditors' pursuit of private profits at almost any cost is not confined either to the financial sector or to the Western world, as is shown in Box 2.3. It is a case of woes wherever the neoliberal model has been adopted.

The pursuit of profits and market shares cannot easily be combined with the audit function. Critics are routinely disarmed with claims that within accounting firms there are Chinese walls that separate the audit and consultancy businesses, but that is not necessarily the case. A US Senate Committee inquiry into the sales of tax avoidance schemes noted

---

Box 2.3 Collusion by auditors in false accounting in Japan

Three auditors from the Japanese firm of ChuoAoyama Pricewater-houseCoopers were given a suspended prison sentence for their role in accounting fraud at Kanebo Ltd, a major cosmetics and textiles company.[29] In 2004, the company admitted to falsifying financial statements for the previous five years and inflating its earnings by around JPY 200 billion (US$1.37 billion; £723 million).[30] Previously, the company reported net assets of JPY 926 million ($7.9 billion) but actually it was over JPY 80 billion in debt. Three auditors helped the company to meet its targets by helping directors to falsify earnings. They not only turned a blind eye to the falsified books and certified them, but also worked with the Kanebo executives to produce false consolidated financial statements to cover up losses. In June 2006, Japanese regulators ordered ChuoAoyama PricewaterhouseCoopers to suspend part of its statutory auditing services for two months. Subsequently, the firm changed its name. But many clients deserted it, it became involved in other scandals, and it was forced to fold its operations.[31]

---

that KPMG's marketing strategies included 'targeting its own audit clients for sales pitches ... KPMG tax professionals were directed to contact existing clients about the product, including KPMG's own audit clients'.[32] The Senate Committee report provided extensive internal documentation to show that the firms deliberately ignored the legal requirements because it calculated that the profits from dubious activities were greater than any possible financial penalties. In 2005, the firm was fined $456 million after admitting 'criminal wrongdoing'.[33] In March 2013, Ernst & Young paid a fine of $123 million after admitting 'wrongful conduct by certain E&Y partners and employees' in selling dubious tax avoidance schemes.[34]

What Is to Be Done

Accountancy firms have been key players in the construction of post-1970s neoliberalism, and are major beneficiaries of the expansion of financial services. They enjoy the state-guaranteed market for external audit, but this monopoly is accompanied by poor regulation and minimal public accountability requirements. So there is little pressure to deliver good audits. Audits are used as a stall for selling other lucrative services, and there is little consideration of any social consequences. The dependence of auditors on their fees from audit clients encourages silence on frauds, fiddles and anti-social practices. In addition the major accounting firms finance and play a major role in the regulatory structures that formulate and monitor accounting and auditing standards. This helps them to advance their business interests and has also helped to keep much needed reform off the political agenda.

The key requirements for any effective reform programme must include:

- the introduction of independent yardsticks for measuring the conduct of an audit
- the opening up of the regulatory process and the investigation of audit failures to effective public scrutiny
- the breaking of the cosy relationship between auditors and their corporate clients
- the development of more direct contact between auditors and the full range of corporate stakeholders that they are supposed to serve
- the imposition of more serious fines and a more serious threat of exclusion from future audit business in the event of any failure to report on misleading or manipulative practices.

3

Avoiding Liability

The avoidance of taxation is not the only major abuse by companies. There have also been repeated cases in which major national and multinational corporations and their directors have managed to avoid liability for disasters and financial losses they have caused throughout the world. This has been achieved by relying on and manipulating three key principles of company law: freedom of incorporation for any purpose, the separate corporate personality of every company so created, and the limited liability that has been granted both to the company and in effect to its directors.

These principles were developed in the United Kingdom in the mid-19th century and have been adopted in almost every jurisdiction throughout the world. Originally it was assumed that incorporation would be restricted to relatively substantial companies with a large number of shareholders who would contribute capital by buying shares, often not paying the full amount at the start in case further calls for more capital were needed. Limited liability was justified at the time as an encouragement for the investment of capital in business enterprises by guaranteeing investors that only what they have invested can be lost and that they will not be required to contribute further from their other assets if the business fails. It also means that directors and executives are generally protected from personal liability to creditors of the company, and thus free to take risks on its behalf.

As in other contexts, however, these principles have been taken advantage of for purposes that were not originally envisaged. As explained in the Introduction, from the 1890s the UK courts accepted that owner directors could shelter behind the separate legal identity of the company they had created and thus avoid personal liability.[1] In the same period, it was accepted in the United States that there was nothing to prevent one company from holding shares in another. These two decisions resulted in two unexpected developments. The first was the proliferation of small one-person companies, often incorporated for tax purposes or to avoid potential personal liability for the debts of insolvent businesses. The second was the proliferation of groups of companies within which very large numbers of subsidiaries could be created in pyramid-like chains. each with its own theoretical independence but in reality owned and controlled by the ultimate holding company at the top of the chain.

These developments opened the way for a number of abusive practices. The combination of limited liability and the separate legal identity of all companies can be taken advantage of to protect questionable or obviously illegitimate methods of business in a wide variety of ways:

- in small companies by protecting those conducting fraudulent or incompetent business operations from any personal liability, including repeated insolvencies in companies established with a view to making money at the expense of creditors and consumers
- by directors and executives of major companies to protect their personal fortunes even when they have been responsible for reckless or grossly incompetent business management
- by those in control of corporate groups to protect the continuing business and assets of the group as a whole from any obligation to pay the debts of an insolvent subsidiary
- by multinationals in creating highly complex corporate groups within which the liability of the holding company or the group as a whole can be protected, for example by setting up subsidiaries or associated companies in jurisdictions in which it is hard to establish or to enforce responsibility.

The first of these is not the main focus of this book, but it can be dealt with not only by disqualification from future directorships, as currently but ineffectively pursued, but by strengthening the procedures for investigating the records of those responsible for the deliberate or repeated corporate insolvencies, imposing personal responsibility and tracking any recoverable assets.

The abuses in larger and more established companies and groups can be illustrated in greater detail.

The fact that most leading bank directors and executives have not been held personally responsible for the huge losses in the recent banking collapses is an obvious example. This stems again from a combination of the separate legal status of the banks and the effective limited liability of directors. Though statutory limited liability is granted only to companies, it extends in practice to their directors and executives. This is because it has long been established that they owe duties of good faith and competence to their companies rather than to their customers, let alone the taxpayers who may have to pay for the costs of bailing out banks and maintaining other essential services. Though the company, and very occasionally share-holders on behalf of 'their' company, may take action against the directors and executives, this is rarely pursued because the remaining or replace-ment directors are usually reluctant to expose themselves to possible future liability. The possibility of a more independent decision arises only when the company has fallen into liquidation or administration, and this is typically avoided by a public or private rescue or takeover. And even if action is taken to recover the losses, the so-called 'business judgement' rule – that directors are not to be held liable for mere misjudgement in commercial matters – makes it difficult to establish liability. Even if it is established, the director's contracts often contain clauses requiring the company to pay the costs of defending any action against them. That leaves only the possibility of a criminal charge, which is likely to be even more difficult to prove unless those responsible have fraudulently diverted company money for their own personal benefit. As a result, as can be seen in Box 3.1, those responsible for huge corporate losses are usually able to walk away with very large severance payments.

What is required to deal with these problems is a clearer and more direct procedure for holding directors and executives to account for irresponsible conduct. Where this results in multi-million-pound losses it may not be possible to recover all the loss from the responsible indi-viduals. However it should be possible to require the repayment of all fees and bonuses paid or payable in the relevant period. That will require some more specific reforms in the law.

The separate corporate personality and limited liability of subsidiaries has often been relied on by their holding companies to avoid liability. One indication of this has been the practice of shipping groups to create a separate company for each of their ships so that in the event of a disaster or liability for delays or accidents they can limit their losses to the remaining value of the ship. The use of subsidiaries in tax avoidance structures, as explained in Chapter 1, is another. Company lawyers and judges and legislation in some jurisdictions have found ways of imposing group liability in some cases (for example where the holding company exercises dominant and direct control over the subsidiary), but this has generally been legally complex and difficult to implement. Rather more impact has often been achieved by activist campaigns against the holding company of major multinationals. Whether in response to these campaigns or an assessment of the reputational damage in commercial circles, their directors have often decided to stand by their subsidiaries on the grounds that walking away from their liabilities would be more damaging than paying up.

---

*Box 3.1   The responsibility and subsequent
fate of some leading bank directors*

Fred Goodwin was the chief executive of Royal Bank of Scotland from 2001 until its collapse and effective nationalisation in 2009. He was responsible for its very rapid expansion, including the purchase of NatWest, Churchill and ABN Amro, funded by massive borrowing and exposing the bank to huge risks in the US subprime mortgage market. By 2009 RBS had accumulated losses of some £240 billion, most of it from the Amro purchase. During his period as CEO Goodwin is estimated to have been paid some £20 million in fees, and on his 'early retirement' he was given a largely discretionary pension pot of £16 million, guaranteeing him an annual pension of £700,000 per year, though following public outrage this was later reduced to £342,000 plus a lump sum of £2.7 million.

Adam Applegarth was the chief executive of Northern Rock, which had been converted from a building society into a bank in 1997. Under his leadership Northern Rock massively increased its mortgage lending, funded by short-term loans on the international market secured on its repackaged mortgages. In 2007 the international market dried up and the Bank of England stepped in with liquid support, triggering a run on the bank by worried depositors and leading to a deficit eventually amounting to some £28 billion. Applegarth resigned in November 2007 with a payoff of £760,000. In its report on Northern Rock the Treasury Select Committee concluded that 'the former directors were the principal authors of its difficulties'.[2]

Halifax Bank of Scotland (HBOS) was managed by Lord Stevenson, Sir James Crosby and Andy Hornby. Despite a warning from its head of Group Regulatory Risk in 2004, which was ignored, the bank had accumulated losses of £10.8 billion by 2008. Though Stevenson and Hornby resigned without a payoff, Hornby moved on to a series of highly paid executive posts in other companies. In 2013 the Parliamentary Banking Standards Commission concluded that the primary responsibility for the losses lay with Stevenson, Crosby and Hornby. It recommended a ban on all three from future involvement in banking, and that 'those responsible for bank failures should be held more directly accountable for their actions'.[3]

There remain some cases in which multinational holding companies have managed to avoid or reduce their liabilities by relying on jurisdictional separation between them and their foreign subsidiaries. The most notorious case was the Bhopal chemical leak, in which the US holding company Union Carbide was able to avoid direct liability for negligent conduct by its Indian subsidiary. When it arranged for the subsidiary to enter into a deal with the Indian government, sanctioned by the Indian courts, many in the most seriously affected communities adjacent to the plant were left without any effective remedy (see Box 3.2).

A more recent example of similar jurisdictional problems, as shown in Box 3.3, has been the way in which Royal Dutch Shell has managed to avoid liability for the human rights abuses resulting from its alleged complicity with the Nigerian government and others in causing massive pollution in the Niger delta. In the United States, as elsewhere, there must now be a need to look for a more modern and comprehensive solution.

A further and more recent avoidance strategy by major Western companies has been to rely on locally incorporated and apparently independent supply companies rather than to establish their own subsidiaries. The recent disasters at jerry-built clothing factories in Bangladesh provide

---

Box 3.2 The Bhopal disaster

Union Carbide (UC), a US corporation, established a chemical production subsidiary, Union Carbide India Ltd (UCIL), in Bhopal in India. UC held 51 per cent of the shares and 49 per cent were held by the Indian government and Indian investors. In 1984 a toxic gas leak led to up to 4,000 immediate deaths and continuing deaths and disabilities to many thousands more. A complex series of actions in both India and the United States led to a ruling in the US courts that the proceedings be transferred to India, on the grounds that UCIL was 'a separate entity, owned, managed and operated exclusively by Indian citizens in India'. The Indian Supreme Court eventually approved the sale of the UC shares to an Indian company, and engineered a settlement under which UC paid US$470 million and undertook to fund a hospital for those affected. The UCIL chairman and chief executive was arrested immediately after the disaster, but was rapidly flown back to the United States. He was later charged with manslaughter but the US authorities refused to extradite him.

Box 3.3 *The United States Alien Tort Claims Act:* Kiobel *v.* Royal Dutch Petroleum

For the past decade many activists in the United States and elsewhere have worked on the idea that multinational corporations can be held accountable for abuses arising from their worldwide operations under the US Alien Tort Claims Act of 1789.[4] This was introduced to allow action to be taken against piracy, but was revived in the 1990s in a series of cases alleging breaches of international human rights by US-based corporations. The initial case was against Unocal, an oil company, for complaints of forcible eviction, murder and other abuses by the Burmese/Myanmar government in the context of a joint venture with Unocal. The case was settled out of court with a substantial payment.

A number of other cases have been pursued, for example against Rio Tinto in respect of abuses during mining operations in Papua New Guinea. The most recent case against Royal Dutch Petroleum centred on the company's alleged complicity with the Nigerian government in compelling its Nigerian subsidiary to cooperate with government forces in suppressing opposition to oil exploration and extraction in the Niger delta. The US Court of Appeal accepted that the Statute did cover abuses of international customary law by individuals, but questioned whether this could be extended to corporations. The US Supreme Court decided unanimously in April 2013 that the Act could not be applied extraterritorially, and effectively ended the potential of this form of litigation against multinationals for abuses in foreign jurisdictions.[5]

---

a striking example. Most international clothing chains claim to be abiding by codes of conduct for the protection of the workers who produce their goods in foreign low-cost jurisdictions. But few are prepared to meet any of the claims for compensation for the local employees killed, injured or made sick by the conditions in the factories where their goods – and their profits – are produced.

There is also a case for curtailing the limited liability enjoyed by the limited liability partnerships (LLPs) now used by hedge funds and others to shield them from potential liability from their short-term trading and corporate 'rescue' operations. The way in which this privilege is used and abused will be explained in Chapter 7, and some remedies will be recommended in Chapter 12.

What Can Be Done About It

- The liability of directors and executives for gross incompetence could be made more effective by providing specifically for the repayment of all fees and bonuses, including share options, paid in respect of the relevant period.
- The continuing attempts to find an answer for the avoidance of liability by corporate groups within standard company law principles – such as the concept of the holding company as a 'shadow director' of all its subsidiaries – have not proved to be workable or effective in many cases.
- A better and more effective approach may be to remove limited liability as such for specified categories of operations, such as certain wholly owned and centrally managed subsidiaries.

4

Extracting Value

Predatory capitalists seek to gain control of valuable corporate assets and extract value for themselves. This is often at the cost of others or the closure of otherwise worthwhile enterprises. In some cases, where the business of the company is to provide essential services, the cost is borne by the taxpayer as the state is effectively obliged to step in to maintain services.

The way in which this is done differs from sector to sector. In some cases, like those of football clubs or care homes, the trick is to take control of an established operating company by some form of leveraged takeover, borrowing a very high proportion of the funds needed to buy the shares and often involving a web of interrelated companies. Cash can then be extracted in various ways – huge management fees, sale and leaseback of valuable assets, or using the company's own assets to finance the borrowing. In others where there is an effective monopoly of services, such as railway franchises, or a risk of systemic damage as in some banking operations, those responsible can simply pay themselves huge salaries and leave the taxpayer to pick up the cost of salvaging the company.

The trouble is that much of this is not technically unlawful, and even when it is against the law, it is often very difficult to prove a criminal offence or to recover any of the cash or assets that have been extracted or disappeared. So prevention is usually better than deterrence by criminalisation or punishment after the event. Some of the problems and what can be done about them can be illustrated by a more detailed look at some recent high-profile cases.

Highly Leveraged Takeovers

Take the case of the Glazer takeover of Manchester United by means of a complex financing scheme which resulted in the debt incurred in acquiring the club having to be repaid out of club finances.[1] Using the assets of a public company to finance the purchase of its own shares is

---

Box 4.1 *The takeover of Manchester United by the Glazers*

Manchester United was highly profitable when it became a public company listed on the Stock Exchange in 1990. Initially all went well. But in 2003 the Glazer family from the United States began to buy shares. By 2004 they had built their holding through Red Football Ltd to just under 30 per cent, which is the level at which a formal takeover bid has to be made. Fortunately for them the Irish financiers John Magner and J. P. McManus had also built a similar stake of 29 per cent. The Glazers bought it and thus gained overall control with 59 per cent of the shares. They continued to buy shares on the market until they had more than 75 per cent, which enabled them to 'go private' by delisting Manchester United from the Stock Exchange. They continued to buy shares until they were entitled to compulsorily purchase the remainder and achieve 100 per cent ownership and control.

All this was financed by massive loans which they were able to secure on the assets of the club as soon as they obtained overall control. Some of the funds were in the form of what are known as PIK (payment in kind) loans at a very high rate of interest (14.25 per cent) which were then sold on to hedge funds through Red Football Joint Venture Ltd, and were secured on that company's shares in Red Football Ltd and thus indirectly on the club's assets. But most of the PIK interest was not actually paid. Instead it was rolled over from year to year until the amount owed was up to £207 million. By early 2010 the total debt had risen to £716 million. In order to pay off the PIK and other loans the Glazers arranged a bond issue for £500 million in mid-2010. The terms of this, however, permitted them to extract £95 million in cash, to pay themselves half of the consolidated net income of the club each year, and to sell and lease back the club's Trafford Training Centre. It is suspected that some at least of these funds were used to pay off the PIK loans, though the club continues to assert that none of the club's money was used to pay off the capital as opposed to the interest.

---

generally supposed to be unlawful.[2] But, as shown in Box 4.1, by using a sophisticated web of interrelated companies, the Glazer family have been able to gain control of what was originally a highly profitable public company, pay themselves handsomely and leave the fans to pay the increased ticket prices that are needed to pay off the £500 million or so of outstanding debt.

The problem here is that the freedom exercised by the Glazers to create a web of separate companies enabled them to get round the simple bar on using the assets of the club to finance its own takeover. By securing the loans for its purchase on the club's assets and then by rolling over the loans when the time for repayment was reached and continuing to pay the interest on them out of the company's income, they achieved precisely that end result. And large amounts continue to be paid to the Glazers personally as management fees and as a proportion of annual profits.

The unanswered question is whether all this was to the benefit of the club and its fans. Could the law and practice of football finance not be regulated to permit and encourage a form of members' club ownership like that of some clubs in Spain and Germany?

Extracting Value by Sale and Leaseback of Assets

A similar means of extracting value is to buy control of a company, sell and lease back its valuable assets and distribute the proceeds of sale to those involved in one form or another. If those involved wish to conceal what they are up to, the property assets can be transferred to separate companies formed for the purpose and then leased back to their original owners on terms that are unduly favourable to those in control of the operation. If those terms result in the original business finding it difficult to maintain the payments, someone else can be left to pick up the pieces.

A shocking example of this, as shown in Box 4.2, was the way in which Castlebeck Care Homes were taken over by the same Irish financiers involved in the Manchester United saga, stripped of its assets and eventually put into liquidation, leaving the care of the long-term residents to local social services while the financiers pocketed the available cash. An even larger sale and lease-back operation resulted in the collapse of the Southern Cross group of care homes in 2011 when local authorities in England cut back on the price they were prepared to pay for private-sector care services. In that case the business model adopted by Southern Cross again resulted in the elderly residents being left at the mercy of predatory financing.

Box 4.2 *The care homes financing scandals*

The ill-treatment of elderly and vulnerable people in private care homes has been widely publicised. The way in which a few Irish financiers managed to extract huge personal profits from care businesses that eventually failed is less well known.

Castlebeck Care Homes, notorious for the abuse of vulnerable inmates by the staff in Winterbourne View, had been bought in 2006 by the Irish financiers J. P. McManus, John Magner and Dermot Desmond for around €316 million. The company was run by Castlebeck Care Ltd, which was a subsidiary of the CB Care Ltd group, which was in turn owned by a Jersey-based company Castle Holdings Ltd, which was controlled by a limited partnership, Lydian Capital Partners, based in Jersey but managed from Geneva. By selling off the property occupied by the care home and leasing it back, the financiers secured and distributed profits for themselves of some £30 million in each of 2009 and 2010. And by arranging for the UK-based operations to be highly indebted – some of the loans were at around 15 per cent interest – they ensured that there would be little or no UK tax due. After the Winterbourne View scandal Castlebeck was sold off, but in the meantime the three Irish millionaires had pocketed huge sums for their personal use.

A similar operation was carried out by the same trio through Barchester Care Homes, also owned by CB Care Ltd, which had bank debts of £233 million and subordinated debts of a further £195 million in 2008–09. The total annual interest of some £38 million left the group with annual losses in 2008 and 2009 of £19 million and £10 million but it still paid the interest of 15 per cent on the subordinated debt, a very good deal for the debt providers.

Vulture Capitalism

A different form of asset stripping is regularly carried out by so-called 'vulture capitalists'. The strategy of the hedge funds involved is to use their cash resources to buy up distressed or bankrupt companies, promising to turn them round. In many cases this involves very substantial downsizing of the business and the disposal of whatever assets can be sold for cash. In some cases a viable but much smaller business is created which can eventually be sold on the market, to another corporate group or in a management buyout. In all these cases the hedge funders can usually manage the affairs of the companies involved in such a way as to ensure they extract large amounts of cash in the process.

A notorious example of this was the purchase of the rump of MG Rover by the Phoenix Consortium. As shown in Box 4.3, the four Phoenix individuals purchased the firm for a mere £10 but over the next five years, until the final collapse of negotiations with potential Chinese buyers, they managed to pay themselves £42 million in executive pay and pensions, leaving an insolvent shell with debts of £1.4 billion. As there is no law against gross overpayment, all attempts to mount a prosecution or to secure any recompense for those who lost their jobs or the taxpayer have so far failed.

Privatised Utilities

The currently prevailing policy of privatising what are essentially monopoly services creates a new and somewhat different opportunity for private sector companies to generate profits for themselves and their shareholders while the long-term risk remains with the taxpayer. The twin objectives of the policy have been to reduce the role of the state in providing services, arguably on more or less ideological grounds, and also to reduce the level of state borrowing, which is a key component of current economic monitoring of state financial stability.

It is now generally accepted that the terms of the private finance initiative (PFI) contracts for the construction of schools and hospitals provided a very attractive means for private sector companies to earn substantial profits over lengthy periods with little or no risk if things went wrong. The commissioning public authorities are contractually obliged to maintain the rental or maintenance payments over the full period of years even if they have no continuing use for the premises, and they are usually unable to avoid maintaining the service if and when things go badly wrong. Most independent economists now believe that it would have been better to fund and provide the necessary buildings or services through long-term public borrowing.

The franchising of the railway network provides some interesting examples of how the system has been manipulated by the private sector companies to produce a continuing flow of income while retaining the ability to hand the operation back to the state if it becomes unprofitable.

Box 4.3 MG Rover and the Phoenix Four

When BMW moved its main Mini operations to Oxford and sold Land Rover to Ford, the remaining parts of MG Rover at Longbridge were making huge losses. The Phoenix Four emerged at the last moment in May 2000 to 'rescue' the operation with a view to finding an international joint venture to secure the future of the plant. They purchased the group for a nominal £10 and were offered a cash dowry of £400 million by BMW to invest in regeneration and a further £75 million as a kind of success fee if they managed to survive.

Over the following five years the Phoenix Four managed to reduce the losses from £400 million in the first eight months of their ownership to £80 million by 2004, partly by reducing production but also by selling off any remaining financially viable parts of the business and eventually the Longbridge plant site itself. They also paid themselves a total of £45 million over the period while they negotiated with a series of potential foreign joint venture partners. But when the Shanghai Automotive Company finally withdrew its interest, MG Rover collapsed in April 2005 with debts of £1.4 billion.

There followed a series of official reports on the disaster by the National Audit Office and others. The report of a massive DTI inquiry[3] in 2009 costing £16 million was referred directly to the Serious Fraud Office, which eventually decided there was no basis for a criminal prosecution, even though the payments from the potential success fee had been concealed by the creation of a separate individually controlled company which received that part of the BMW funding in loan notes. The DTI report concluded that there had been little justification for the level of payments made by the Phoenix Four to themselves, and that there had been serious failures in corporate governance. But the only formal action was a subsequent disqualification of the four from future directorships.

The franchise awarded to National Express to run the East Coast line from London to Scotland, as shown in Box 4.4, is particularly relevant since it demonstrates how separate corporate structures may be used to isolate less profitable from more profitable operations. It also illustrates how the ideological commitment to franchising in this way has taken precedence over a more rational and less costly economic model.

Box 4.4 The East Coast railway franchise fiasco

The franchise for the East Coast railway was awarded to a National Express subsidiary in 2007 for seven and a half years in return for a promised payment to the Treasury of £1.4 billion. After only two years the subsidiary threatened to withdraw, as its revenues were declining, and National Express refused to provide the necessary financial support. A National Audit Office report[4] concluded that the subsidiary's business plan was not sustainable and that the Department of Transport was faced with a choice between renegotiation or termination. It also stated that there was no obligation on the National Express holding company, which held other profitable franchises, to support its subsidiary. The Department chose termination, at an estimated loss of some £350 million to the end of 2012, as it feared that if it agreed to renegotiate the terms other franchisees would also seek to reopen their deals. A not-for-profit public company was established to operate the line and has been running it more successfully than National Express. Despite this the Tory/Lib Dem coalition embarked on a renewed franchise offering in 2013, which has been further delayed as a result of inaccurate Departmental financial assessments.

What Can Be Done About These Practices

The current legal rules are clearly inadequate to control or prevent these predatory practices. Some legal reforms might be made to curtail the most obvious manipulations:

- The bar on using a company's assets to fund the purchase of its own shares could be strengthened to include the roundabout avoidance structures used by some financiers.
- The provisions governing excessive self-authorised executive pay could be strengthened, as has already been promised by the current Tory/Lib Dem coalition, though as argued in other chapters their proposals are unlikely to make much difference. A more radical proposal to restrict executive pay increases to prescribed levels would be more effective.[5]
- A different approach to the regulation of corporate structures is needed for football clubs (to encourage and facilitate fan-based ownership).

- Different structures are also required, as argued in Chapter 14, for care homes, railway services and other such enterprises that are substantially funded, though indirectly, at national or local government expense (to ensure more effective regulation of financial models that encourage excessive debt and associated tax avoidance).

5

Managerial Self-Interest

The remorseless advance of managerial self-interest is the cause of much anger among other stakeholders. Levels of remuneration for bankers and corporate bosses have continued their dramatic upsurge, while the pay of others has either been severely constrained or discontinued altogether. The resulting levels of inequality, especially in Anglo-American economies, are unprecedented and will almost certainly have to be brought under some form of control, one way or another.

A simple measure of managerial self-interest is the ratio of top management remuneration to that of the lowest-paid workers in the same company. This is not an accurate measure as it can be difficult to apply a monetary value to some managerial benefits, such as the satisfaction of performing an interesting and worthwhile job, rather than the boring repetition of some unskilled labour. Nonetheless, this is a reasonable proxy for a measure of managerial self-interest. As Plato (427–347 BC) recognised, social cohesion can be threatened by a sense of social injustice, and he considered that a fourfold difference between the highest-paid and the lowest-paid was within the limits of acceptability. In the 20th century, the banker J. P. Morgan argued that top executives should earn no more than 20 times the pay of those at the bottom. This view was supported by Peter Drucker, the eminent management thinker, who believed that top executives paid more than that would not be able to manage their firms effectively, as it would inflict untold damage on morale by unleashing 'the hatred, contempt and even fury' of the mass of employees and other citizens.[1] What might they have to say about the multiple of chief executive pay to average pay (which is obviously higher than the lowest pay) for UK FTSE 100 companies, which during the decade to 2010 moved from 69 times to 149 times? In the United States, in 2010 the average multiple of chief executive officer (CEO) compensation over pay for rank-and-file workers in S&P 500 Index companies reached 204, up 20 per cent since 2009.

Striking examples of the ratio between top executives and the people they employ include Bart Becht, CEO of Reckitt Benckiser, the FTSE

100's highest paid boss, who received £37 million in 2009, or 1,374 times as much as Reckitt's average worker. Nick Buckles, CEO of G4S, was paid 328 times the company's average staff salary, while Sir Terry Leahy, Tesco's then CEO, was paid more than 900 times as much as the average Tesco worker.

Payment for Incompetence and Criminality

This is not just about ratios. Within the broader picture of remuneration, there have been many individual instances of outrageous excess that have sparked media attention and public anger. This is especially the case when excessive remuneration is unrelated to performance. A striking example is the final payment of £1.2 million to Nick Buckles, who presided over G4S's London Olympics security shambles and whose obvious incompetence eventually forced his exit. Both G4S and fellow outsourcing contractor Serco have been referred to the Serious Fraud Office for investigation of allegations of overcharging and fraud on 22 out of 28 tenders won from government departments and agencies. Nevertheless, Serco awarded CEO Christopher Hyman a pay-rise to £779,000 on top of his performance share plan worth an extra £1.5 million, and a more than generous pension pot.

The boundaries between pure self-interest, competence and straightforward criminality are not, of course, black and white. Like the distinctions between tax avoidance and evasion, there are shades of grey which may have to be identified at considerable expense in courts of law or official inquiries, or left indistinct and exploitable. The levels of payments in the banking and financial sectors are notoriously excessive, as shown in Box 5.1.

These too seem to be regarded as unrelated to any concept of legitimate or lawful business success. Each of these four examples can be linked to clear evidence of illegitimate or unlawful conduct in the company while these individuals were in charge, as shown in Box 5.2.

Conduct and payments like this now appear almost customary in the banking world. In recent years, most major banks have paid unimaginably huge fines, rather than face charges for fraudulent activity. *The Economist's* description of 'casual dishonesty' seems scarcely appropriate to conduct that was clearly an essential and endemic part of the business models that produced the massive profits from which the payments were made.

---

*Box 5.1 Headline examples of huge payments
to four 'masters' of the financial sector*

The Times of 26 March 2007 headlined that rewards for Barclays' Bob Diamond had hit more than £80 million; it reported that the bank's president and boss of Barcap collected £15.2 million in salary and perks.

Glencore CEO Ivan Glasenberg, billionaire recipient from Glencore's initial public offering, received a further £71 million dividend in 2011 from his Glencore shares which were part of his personal take from the IPO.

Blackstone boss Stephen Schwarzman took $213.3 million in pay and cash dividends in 2012, slightly down on the $213.5 million he received the previous year.

JP Morgan Chase CEO Jamie Dimon received $18.7 million in compensation in 2012, down 19 per cent from his 2011 $23 million pay.

Executive Motivations

Corporate executives appear driven to explore every possibility for making money for their company, for example through the exploitation of loopholes to avoid tax, and thus to enrich themselves. The culture which is currently dominant undeniably serves the purpose of maximising managerial self-interest. But is managerial self-interest really the driving force? Or is there more to the establishment and protection of this casually or systematically dishonest culture?

The obvious first question is 'why do these exploitative, predatory activities occur?' The equally obvious answer is 'because they can'. Human beings are intrinsically motivated to achieve worthwhile objectives, but with few exceptions they are corruptible. Given the option of taking an annual salary of £25,000 or £1 million, most of us would choose £1 million. But there might be strings attached. Most of us would wish to examine those strings and consider our actions. As Zurich University economist Bruno Frey argued in his economic theory of personal motivation, extrinsic, especially monetary, rewards have the effect of 'crowding out' and undermining intrinsic motivations.[2] Most of us are vulnerable

---

Box 5.2   *Headline examples of illegitimate or unlawful conduct by their companies*

Barcap boss Bob Diamond presided over the criminal LIBOR rate-fixing scandal in what *The Economist* referred to as a 'culture of casual dishonesty', but was nevertheless promoted to CEO of the whole bank.

Glencore, the world's largest commodity trader, which is listed in London but successfully avoids paying UK taxes, acquired an associate company, Xstrata, giving the combine sufficient power to fix the supply, and therefore prices, of strategic minerals such as nickel, zinc, platinum, chrome and copper, as well as being highly influential in thermal and coking coal, and in grain markets, which it had previously been widely reported as 'fixing'. Glencore's problem is to judge just how much profit it should take – if they took too much, there might be a serious reaction.

Blackstone Group LP, the world's biggest private equity firm, which is led by ex-Lehman Brothers executives, including CEO Schwarzman, was the firm which, among many other things, stripped the now bankrupt Southern Cross healthcare group of its main assets and property, and made off with an estimated £500 million.

In the final quarter of 2013, JP Morgan Chase agreed settlement of a $13 billion fine for fraud and criminality carried out while Jamie Dimon was in control.

---

to the seductions of monetary rewards, which debase 'moral values such as truth, trust, acceptance, restraint, obligation and tend to reduce the intrinsic motivation to perform'.[3]

Frey's analysis suggests that intrinsic motivations of people working in companies, whatever those motivations might be, are vulnerable to the crowding-out effect if the individuals are presented with the opportunity for monetary rewards. On this analysis, the only difference between the Diamonds, Glasenbergs, Dimons, Schwarzmans and Hymans of the financial world and the rest of us is that their intrinsic motivations have been crowded out already. They have been corrupted. The rest of us are still waiting.

Ideas about human beings' intrinsic motivation have not progressed hugely from the notions first explicated by Adam Smith. He outlined a hierarchy of motivations. The first need was for food. When that was satisfied, the motivation was to obtain 'other wants and fancies of mankind: clothing and lodging, household furniture and what is called equipage'.[4] Beyond those predictable motivations some argued that pleasure, vice and luxury are a more effective driver of economic progress, but Smith suggested that frugality was more powerful. By frugality he meant that which enabled people to become 'proper objects of this respect, of deserving and obtaining this credit and rank among our equals'.[5] As Frey suggests, Smith's concerns have been crowded out by the monetisation of human motivation suggested by neoclassical economic ideology.

The results of the excesses of managerial self-interest appear to lack sustainable benefit to the economy, national or global, nor do they contribute to the common good. Moreover, their divisiveness makes it likely and perhaps inevitable that at some stage they will be reversed, by either regulation or revolution. If the excesses of managerial self-interest are in no one else's interest, why is it that they are not stopped?

Moderating Excess

Actions to moderate these excesses have been proposed. In the United States, Congress ordered public companies to reveal actual CEO-to-worker pay ratios.[6] The Securities and Exchange Commission (SEC) appears to have accepted that it should require companies to report the ratio every year, and has suggested no more than 100:1 is appropriate. However, the SEC has not yet implemented such a rule. It has been vehemently opposed by the US Chamber of Commerce. Corporations and their agents have lobbied energetically against such a proposal on the grounds that it would be too costly to compile and not useful for investors. Real progress in reining in excess has been slow in the United States, despite the legalistic approach taken.

In the United Kingdom, the approach to moderating excess has been deliberately voluntarist and focused more on the issue of codes of best practice governance, rather than legal requirements with specified consequences for non-compliance. Companies are required to comply or explain why they do not comply with the code, with limited guidance over what an appropriate explanation might comprise. The 2010 UK Corporate Governance Code asserts that 'levels of remuneration should be sufficient to attract, retain and motivate directors of the quality required to run the company successfully, but a company should avoid paying more than is necessary for this purpose'. In addition, it suggests that remuneration should be linked to performance, and that the remuneration of the chairperson and executive directors should be set by a remuneration committee comprising non-executive directors. The ostensible independence of committee members is a crucial characteristic which should take remuneration beyond the direct control of the company's executives. But real independence is difficult to assess and maintain. Remuneration committee members might be apparently independent non-executive directors but many of them are executive directors of another company which displays a similar approach to compliance with the code of practice. A degree of mutual interest in exchanging remuneration committee members is likely to grow up and tear away the fig-leaf independence.

It seems that in both the United States and the United Kingdom, care is taken to ensure that the rules are discussed but they are perhaps not intended to be implemented too energetically. Such initiatives appear more as window-dressing cover for 'business as usual'. The reason is open to conjecture. Is it a conspiracy of the plutocrats against the rest? Or is it a genuine, if misplaced, belief in a false economic ideology?

False Economic Theory

The core of the economic theory which seeks to explain self-interest is the idea of 'economic man', a concept shaped as part of neoclassical economics and its reliance on mathematical models to explain economic actors, structures and transactions. This currently dominant ideology depicts people as seeking only to maximise their own self-interest, which can only, for arithmetic calculation, be expressed in monetary terms.

The underlying economic logic stems from Adam Smith, who acknowledged it was 'not from the benevolence of the butcher, the brewer, or the baker, that we expect our dinner, but from their regard for their own interest'.[7] For Smith's artisans that self-interest was to provide a life-long means of support for themselves and their dependants.

The form of self-interest later elaborated by mathematical economists was turned into a maximisation function: maximising profit. This completely changed its character. Maximisation of one thing necessarily implies the impoverishment of everything else, with a resulting focus on the immediate and short term.

The decisive importance of maximisation was achieved by its conversion from maximising profit, which was potentially at least for the benefit of all company stakeholders, to maximising shareholder wealth. This was first enunciated by Milton Friedman in 1962, as being the only social responsibility of corporate officials.[8] The result has been the impoverishment of other stakeholders and the prioritising of the short term over longer-term interests.

Electricity distributor UKPN provides a typical example – there are many more – of a perfectly legal business in which massive increases in the CEO's remuneration were a small price to pay for his complicity in the process of maximising shareholder wealth, as shown in Box 5.3.

There was initially limited theoretical justification for the changed focus from profit to what became known as shareholder value, other than a weak assertion regarding 'residual beneficiaries'. The argument was that all other stakeholders, such as lenders, suppliers, customers and employees, were guaranteed their repayment by the company and therefore could not be said to have taken any risk in their dealings with the company. Only the shareholders bore risk, and they were therefore entitled to all the residual return after those other stakeholders had received their guaranteed amounts. That argument is false in several respects. The other stakeholders are not risk-free in their dealings with the company. Employees are not guaranteed employment. Nor are suppliers guaranteed payment. Nor are lenders to the company guaranteed the repayment of their loans. Moreover, it is obvious that employees place far more at risk with the company than simply a discretionary monetary investment.

A theoretical justification for maximising shareholder wealth was later

---

Box 5.3 UK Power Networks (UKPN)

The highly profitable UKPN cut its workforce by 300 in 2012 and was unable to protect its customers from storm damage, leaving more than 300,000 homes without power over Christmas 2013, some for as long as five days. The company is owned by Hong Kong based Li Ka-shing, and carries £4.7 billion of debt on its balance sheet, more than 80 per cent of its 2010 acquisition cost. In 2012 UKPN made profits of £939 million, almost 20 per cent up on 2011. It paid its CEO, Basil Scarsella, a salary of £1.4 million and £270,000 in bonus and pension payments, and returned £135 million in dividends to its parent companies registered in Hong Kong and the offshore tax havens Bermuda and the British Virgin Islands. UKPN paid corporation tax at a rate of just 10.2 per cent in 2012.

invented by theoretical economists misusing the concept of agency, a legal relationship which dates back to the earliest overseas trading expeditions. In those days, the ship's captain was deemed to be the agent of those financing the expedition, who were its principals. The captain was therefore enabled to enter legally binding agreements on their behalf, at the same time being required at all times to act professionally in their best interests. Agency theory asserts that company directors, like the ship's captain of old, are the agents of the shareholders, rather than of the company. This is palpably false. Directors and executives are agents of the company, and have always been treated as such since joint stock companies were first established as separate legal entities. Company directors were and are still specifically contracted to act for and on behalf of the company and in its best interests at all times. Directors, like all other employees, have contracts of employment directly with the company, not with the shareholders.

For agency theory to be valid, it would be necessary to deny the company its legal existence. Some much-cited academic papers have endeavoured to establish this, claiming that the company is merely a 'centralised contractual agent in a team productive process',[9] or more simply 'a legal fiction'.[10] The Institute of Economic Affairs even went so far as to publish a paper claiming that though the company was a legal entity, it was in effect a 'slave' without legal rights.[11] In fact company legislation across the world accords the company or corporation a separate legal existence, with rights to make contracts and behave in many ways like a person, with directors acting for and on its behalf. Successive Companies Acts have made clear the duty of directors to act on behalf of the company and in its best interests at all times. There is only one recorded example of case law, from the Supreme Court of Michigan in 1919, which supports the agency theory idea, and that was so weak a precedent that it has only been cited once in court.[12]

The argument for maximising shareholder wealth at the expense of all other stakeholders therefore lacks both legal and theoretical support. However, acting against the interests of the company for the sole gain of shareholders has not yet been tested in courts of law as a criminal offence.

The Power of False Theory

Agency theory, though false, has been generally accepted, and it has resulted in massive gains for the owners of capital. It has been lobbied for and promulgated by agencies such as the US Business Roundtable and the CBI in the United Kingdom, and has been taught in business schools across the globe as an essential element of neoclassical ideology. Consequently, it has become the universally accepted orthodoxy which continues to drive the industrial–financial–political nexus.

Theorists have reinforced the practical consequences of the false theory by focusing on what they identify as the 'agency problem' – which is that directors and managers, as examples of economic man, act in their own interests rather than as agents of shareholders. The solution has been to convert them into shareholders through the provision of the share option bonus schemes which have generated so much of the remuneration excesses outlined above. Much merger and acquisition activity, as well as the stock buy-backs and other initiatives to extract value dealt with in the previous chapter, is driven by this logic. The example of Cadbury's takeover by Kraft was a stark reminder of its power. Cadbury was a strong, high-performing company with a proud history and culture. Its directors' legal duties were to act in the company's best interests at all times. They might have reasonably been expected to be motivated to the company's long-term success. However, when Cadbury received a takeover bid from Kraft, the general belief was that Cadbury's directors should recommend the sale of the company because it provided shareholders with a windfall gain that would have taken several years to achieve by other means. All they had to do was to maximise the price Kraft would pay. Chief executive Todd Stitzer received a £12 million bonus for recommending the sale of the company. Even that was not widely thought to be evidence of any conflict of interest between him and the Cadbury company. No mention was made in the considerable press coverage that the Cadbury directors had been corrupted, or acted in any way that was improper or inappropriate.

It appears that managerial self-interest is a means to the end of maximising shareholder wealth. It is not the real driving force behind the explosion of inequality and inequity, but the monetary crowding out of management's intrinsic motivations, in effect the corruption of management, is a significant and false step towards maximising shareholder wealth and impoverishing all else. The real driving force is the falsely based but genuine belief in an economic ideology that is deliberately promoted by its plutocratic beneficiaries.

What Needs To Be Done About It

If these practices and their supporting ideologies are to be altered for the better, here are some of the things that will need to be included:

- reversal of the academy's singular promulgation of neoclassical economic theory, including especially repudiation of agency theory, and return to a more pluralistic approach to economic understanding and research
- reinforcement of the legal duty of directors to pursue the long-term interests of the company for all its stakeholders
- requirement for the genuine independence of remuneration committee members, who must also include representatives of employees
- a legal requirement to report on salary ratios, top to bottom
- effective controls on success fees in the context of takeovers and mergers
- review of the practical impact of managerial bonus schemes.

6

The Mirage of Corporate Social Responsibility

The corporation's focus on maximising shareholder value at the expense of all other objects is constrained only by voluntary codes of practice and the limitations which might, or might not, be imposed by problematic law. It is not currently required that the common good, the environment or the interests of future generations should limit the shareholder value seeking behaviour of the corporation. However, it may be in the corporation's best business interest to be seen to ensure that its behaviour is socially responsible. Corporate social responsibility (CSR) refers to the many and various self-regulatory mechanisms and controls which corporate management might initiate to ensure, or be seen to ensure, compliance with ethical standards, international norms and the true spirit of the law, in transactions with all stakeholders.

In 1958 Theodore Levitt warned in the pages of the *Harvard Business Review* about 'the dangers of social responsibility'.[1] The idea that companies should exercise responsibilities beyond that of making money was becoming fashionable, and Levitt's warning was intended for the future of both capitalism and the corporation. Chandler had identified the corporation as 'the most powerful institution in the American economy and its managers the most influential group of economic decision makers'.[2] Levitt's contention was that the business of business was making profit, not 'sweet music'.

At the time of Levitt's warning, the struggle between capitalism and socialism was at its height. Economists such as von Mises and Hayek of the Austrian School argued that any step taken in the direction of socialism would lead inexorably to a full-on centrally planned totalitarian communist state. The Austrian approach was later popularised by Milton Friedman,[3] focusing on maximised shareholder value and a minimised state. It became the utterly dominant economic orthodoxy in Anglo-American economies, just as the threat of socialism was beginning to dissolve in the 1980s. It has since been promulgated by the pro-business community in Britain and America, including for example the CBI in Britain and the Business Roundtable in the United States, as well as myriad corporate lobbyists, think-tanks and consultants, amply financed by private corporate sources.

The self-regulatory role of CSR has retained prominence, both as a subject area taught in business schools and university departments, and as a focus for practitioner activity. But there remains a fundamental ambiguity in CSR's role and intent. It is a means of both legitimising the capitalist corporation and genuinely modifying corporate behaviour, but it may also be just a form of public relations window-dressing, aimed at persuading the corporation's stakeholders. Depending on context, it may have substance or it may be a mirage.

The Development of Corporate Social Responsibility

These are the shifting sands on which attempts to promote CSR have been built. There is a long history of initiatives oriented towards social responsibility which have sought to modify the behaviour of corporations. Khurana recounted how the first US business schools sought to establish the control of big business by management as a profession, with professional expertise and responsibilities as well as commitments to standards of behaviour and integrity.[4] This was based on the approach of other professions such as medicine and the law. The crucial difference was that the medical and legal professions could control entry qualifications and continuing standards of performance and behaviour. Failure to conform would in principle lead to exclusion from the profession. Management clearly had no such effective gatekeeper. Successful entrepreneurs could create important management roles and responsibilities for themselves. The business schools were clearly unable to establish management as a profession. So they focused on developing professional expertise, and a formulation of professional values which sought to mimic those encapsulated by the medical profession's Hippocratic Oath.

Management expertise as taught in business schools has invariably included concern for both efficiency and equitable values. The emphasis has moved from one to the other as the ideological mainstream focus shifts from the balance among all stakeholders to the exclusive focus on shareholder interests. When shareholder value is dominant, the emphasis is inevitably on efficiency, with social responsibility becoming largely a matter of window-dressing and public relations. When equitable values are driving what J. K. Galbraith referred to as social balance, then social responsibility becomes a serious and genuine pursuit.

Concentration on shareholder value encourages corporate management to push against all the legal boundaries, giving rise to many notorious cases of fraud and criminality. The Committee on the Financial Aspects of Corporate Governance, chaired by Adrian Cadbury, identified the prevention of corporate crime as a prime motivation, listing as key examples the Guinness share-trading fraud, Robert Maxwell's corporate and pension fund thefts, and the Bank of Credit and Commerce International's frauds and thefts involving drug dealing and money laundering.[5]

The Committee's 1992 Cadbury Report proposed the first Code of Best Practice on corporate governance. It was followed by many others across the globe. The two essential characteristics of such codes are that they are voluntary and that their wording is ambiguous and therefore open to interpretation. The injunction has been to 'comply or explain' why you are not complying, but this would only be a strong motivator for behaviour if non-compliant explanations were subjected to rigorous analysis and reporting. This is rarely done. Explanations can be woefully inadequate or simply not given at all, without repercussions of any kind.

Clause 1.3 of the Cadbury code is a typical example of ambiguity: 'The board should include non-executive directors of sufficient calibre and number for their views to carry significant weight in the board's decisions.' Interpretation of this clause is wide open to argument about its true intended meaning. The concept of 'sufficient calibre' is famously problematic. A safe way of ensuring that non-executive directors are of sufficient calibre is to appoint those who have already been assessed and appointed as executive directors of other companies. The requirement thus encourages a closed shop of mutually compliant directors, reducing the practical effect of non-executive directors being independent, particularly in their roles on remuneration and audit committees.

The weakness of the Code became clear in the financial crash of 2007–08. The conduct of many companies and their boards of directors involved not just a perfectly legal, but extreme, focus on shareholder value, but also elements of fraud and criminality. The inevitable result was the impoverishment of all other interests. The resulting damage has been immense, not just to the current global population as a result of an avoidable recession, but to future generations for whom the present population bears some responsibility.

This is the current context that has provoked serious reconsideration of the role for CSR initiatives. CSR is about a company's responsibilities to society, which are now better understood than ever before. Exclusive focus on shareholder value has been shown to be a major cause of increasing social inequality. Knowledge about the impact of the corporate economy on the environment and ecosystems, and therefore on Earth's climate and species, is continuously increasing. There can now be limited room for denial of the reality of climate change, its likely impacts and its causes. CSR is intended to provide a framework for companies and their directors and managers to act responsibly in addressing these problems in the interests both of today's society and tomorrow's. That necessarily includes consideration of the company's direct interactions with members of that society, notably including its employees.

CSR establishes objective measures of managerial behaviour and responsibility with respect to all stakeholders, and requires regular public reporting on whether and how they have been achieved. Within this framework the ethics of management practice remains a matter of choice within the law. Governance is self-regulated. Businesses monitor their own performance, reporting that performance as they see fit, and ensuring its compliance within their own definition of the spirit of the law and their assessment of accepted ethical standards.

Under this voluntarist regime CSR seems likely to have a highly variable impact on corporate practice. In some companies CSR may achieve profound results in terms of corporate behaviour, while in others it may merely provide cover for maintaining business as usual.

The case of BP, as shown in Box 6.1, illustrates the fundamental ambiguity inherent in CSR, and the variable meaning and value of the statements in CSR reports. Those in ultimate charge of major corporate groups should be able to control for the sort of persistent safety violations and legal transgressions which have occurred in BP's recent operations. The fact that they have not managed to do so might arise because firms as large and complex as BP are too big to manage. Heffernan has flagged up BP's problems of size, complexity and distance, with the result that its top executives never engage with those in direct charge of operations except by occasional videoconferencing.[6] In practice BP management was the victim of structural blindness in which 'the bubble of power seals off bad news, inconvenient details, hostile opinions, and messy realities, leaving you free to inhale the rarefied air of pure abstraction'.[7]

This structural blindness is increasingly relevant in the global context in which major corporations like BP are able to dominate their business sectors in both developed and maturing markets. And their corporate reports are audited and approved by similar 'big four' market dominant accountancy firms. Arthur Anderson, the fifth of the 'big five', was closed down following its criminal behaviour when acting as auditor to the

---

Box 6.1 The case of BP: operational reality and CSR reporting

The Texas City refinery explosion, 2005

The refinery explosion killed 15 workers and injured more than 170. Subsequent investigations identified numerous technical and organisational failings both locally and through the company. BP was charged with criminal violations of federal environmental laws, given record fines for safety violations, and subsequently an even larger fine for failure to implement safety improvements following the disaster.

The Deepwater Horizon oil spill, 2010

The explosion and sinking of the oil rig claimed eleven lives, and for 87 days leaked an estimated 4.9 million barrels of oil into the Gulf of Mexico, wreaking extensive damage to marine and wildlife habitats, fishing and tourism industries, as well as the health of clean-up workers and local residents. The US Government report found BP responsible because of over-aggressive cost-cutting and inadequate safety systems. The company settled criminal and civil charges out of court, setting around $40 billion aside to pay these costs.

continued opposite

---

fraudulent energy giant Enron. Similar structural blindness no doubt affected banker JP Morgan Chase which had, by 2014, paid fines of around $20 billion for criminal and fraudulent behaviour.

At the opposite extreme in terms of size, complexity and distance, Ben & Jerry's ice cream was started in 1978 by Ben Cohen and Jerry Greenfield. The Ben & Jerry's Foundation was established in 1985, funded by 7.5 per cent of the company's annual pre-tax profits and supported various socially responsible community-oriented initiatives. Also, in the interests of safety for consumers and the environment, the company opposed the use of a bovine growth hormone to boost milk production. It joined a co-operative campaign with the national non-profit Children's Defense Fund to publicise children's basic needs. For Ben & Jerry's CSR appeared to be real. Then in 2000, the business was acquired by food giant Unilever, which claimed the intention was to carry on engaging with 'these critical, global, economic and social missions'. The company's 2014 mission statement includes a social mission, which includes 'initi-

BP's public relations initiatives

These two major incidents have been a public relations disaster for BP. The stories are too big to hide, so the company has invested hugely in its online image by managing negative search results. For instance a search on 'BP oil spill' produces results focused on the financial impact of the spill, and debate over responsibility for the spill 'which leaves doubt as to whether BP deserves the blame'.[8] This is probably the best possible result for BP.

BP's CSR-related statements, 2013

Sustainability: BP is working to enhance safety and risk management, grow value and build trust. We believe we have a positive role to play in shaping the long-term future of energy.

Our people and values: We value diversity of people and thought, and we aim to make sure that everyone at BP is treated with respect and dignity.

Safety: Safety is a priority for us and we continue working to embed safety and operational risk management into the heart of the company.

Environment: BP is working to manage the environmental impacts of our operations and projects wherever we do business.[9]

ating innovative ways to improve the quality of life locally, nationally, and internationally!' A product mission includes commitment to 'incorporating wholesome, natural ingredients and promoting business practices that respect the earth and the environment'.[10]

There is an essential ambiguity about the CSR culture, just as there is about the 'comply or explain' approach of codes of practice. The mechanisms and processes of CSR can be adopted either as a determined attempt to shape corporate behaviour for the common good, or as a form of PR window-dressing which corporations are expected to present, as is implied by the BP case.

While the dominant mainstream ideology remains committed to maximising shareholder value, the actual delivery of CSR seems likely to be mostly reduced to PR window-dressing, the mirage. If social balance and concern for the common good were to become mainstream, then

CSR might be reinvested with real value. Until such a change takes place CSR will remain without real practical substance.

However, it may be more serious than that. The CSR culture may comprise processes and systems which are deliberately initiated to protect corporations from too searching an analysis of their unethical practices, and thus to avoid any consequent restrictive regulation or legislation. In such cases, CSR may be simply a small part of the neoclassical mainstream aimed at maintaining the status quo rather than its improvement.

What Needs To Be Done

The ideological context of corporate activity swings from one extreme position to another, from overwhelming concern for social responsibilities and balance, to a dominant and exclusive focus on shareholder value. The swing back from shareholder value seems to have already begun, and there is no reason to suppose that oscillation will cease. The worth and effect of initiatives such as CSR can also change from something almost trivial, little more than window-dressing in one context, to something valuable and effective in the opposite setting. There is every reason to expect that movement to continue.

The pendulum in 2014 appears to be starting its return, with an increasing anger over the excesses of the plutocrats and raised concern for the common good. A sustainable business model, enforcing a reduced focus on maximising shareholder value, is beginning to emerge. The mainstream will have to incorporate CSR and make it work. Levitt warned of the dangers of social responsibility because he did not foresee the dangers of corporate social irresponsibility, which are so obvious today.

Changes will have to be made to improve the social responsibility of business:

- First and foremost, the law as it stands must be rigorously enforced. Directors routinely ignore the requirement in the Companies Act 2006 to act in the best long-term interests of the company, not the shareholders, having regard to the interests of all stakeholders. Acting in any other way is illegal and should be punished.
- Stakeholder interests include the environment as proxy for future generations. It is vitally important that companies are made responsible for their own externalised costs, in the form of for example pollution

and wasted finite resources. Punitive fines must be imposed on those evading that responsibility.

- Codes of practice need to be strengthened to include considerations beyond just the financial aspects of governance. For companies whose shares are traded on a stock market, the code must be made mandatory, rather than subject to 'comply or explain', and the consequences for non-compliance be made punitive.

In that revised context, CSR will have a real and useful role to play, ensuring the corporation is not punished for avoidable transgression.

7

Bad Banking and Market Manipulation

Corporate abuses and self-interested conduct have been especially prevalent in the banking and financial sectors. Reckless lending by the largest banks, reckless speculation in complex financial instruments in their investment banking operations, and manipulation and arbitrage in the financial markets have distorted the British economy and played a major role in precipitating the financial crisis of 2008. This has severely decreased the potential for productive investment, opened up new forms of exploitation and illegality, and contributed to greater social and economic inequality. This chapter explains the ways in which these financial abuses were allowed – or encouraged – to take root, and points towards the range of fundamental reforms of the financial sector that will be required to make it fit to support a more stable corporate economy and a fairer society, as will be set out in Part II.

The Big Banks and Their Role in Shaping the Dynamics of the Financial Market

The UK Stock Exchange before the 'big bang' in 1986 consisted of a number of small private partnerships with very distinctive roles in the system. Brokers bought and sold shares on behalf of their clients; they did so from jobbers on the floor of the Stock Exchange. Membership was confined to a limited number of these firms. Behaviour in this context was monitored by peers. This was still the era of 'gentlemanly capitalism' when the City was dominated mainly by people educated in the same public schools and universities, attending the same Establishment social events and connected through family, friendship or long-term business connections.[1] The City was in turn overseen by the Bank of England, which acted as ultimate protector of these institutions both against their own greed and stupidity, and against possible government intervention.[2]

Over a period of time, deregulation broke this system apart. It enabled the entry of foreign financial institutions, particularly the US investment banks, whose scale and scope became a model for their UK and European competitors. These institutions brought new capital into the City as well as new corporate structures and practices. At first, British authorities sought to continue the tradition of self-regulation even in these changed circumstances. By the late 1990s, however, a more formal system of regulation was developing, but it was one which still remained 'light touch' and dependent on insiders. There was still a belief that insiders could best look after their own affairs, and that this would allow financial innovation and growth of the market, whose established mechanisms would ensure that abuses could not develop or would be rapidly revealed.[3] Thus the big financial institutions were far freer in London to develop new products and processes than they were even in the United States where the New Deal legislation of the 1930s continued to constrain what banks could do.

As a result, London became an important site for the large US investment banks, such as Goldman Sachs, Lehman Brothers, JP Morgan, and Merrill Lynch. It also attracted large banks from Europe, where traditions of universal banking meant that in economies like France, Germany and Switzerland there were large powerful banks operating in both retail and wholesale banking, such as Deutsche Bank, BNP-Paribas, UBS and Credit Suisse. However, the tight regulations in their home countries on how financial markets could develop meant that if they wanted to grow as rapidly as the US banks they had to set up operations in London and New York. Thus both US and European banking giants moved into London to take advantage of what was known politely as 'self-regulation' and of the rapid growth of its financial markets. By the early 2000s London had completely changed from its pre-'big bang' structure. It was dominated by a relatively small number of US investment banks, a group of large universal banks from Germany, France and Switzerland with strong investment banking businesses and ambitions, and a small number of UK-based institutions such as HSBC and Barclays. For most of the 2000s Barclays under the leadership of Bob Diamond was the most active and aggressive of these UK firms in the wholesale market.

In the period before 'big bang' most of the operators in the financial markets had been partnerships where individuals risked their own wealth if they made the wrong decisions. Now most of these large financial institutions were publicly owned limited liability companies which increasingly sought to maximise shareholder returns.[4] In the traditional model of banking, known as 'fractional reserve banking', a bank takes money in from its depositors, and depositors receive interest on the balances in their accounts, which they can take out at any time. The bank lends money using these deposits as security, usually for longer fixed terms and for higher rates of interest. The bank keeps a fraction of its cash in reserve in case depositors want their money back. If, in exceptional circumstances, lots of depositors want their money back at the same time and there is a 'run on the bank', the bank looks to the central bank – the Bank of England in the United Kingdom – to help it over the problem by swapping long-term assets for cash, enabling it to pay back its depositors. In this traditional 'fractional reserve banking' system, profitability was based on the simple difference in interest rates that the bank could maintain.

Other areas of the City were predominantly controlled by small partnership firms with limited risk capital, which generally relied on fees for their intermediary services rather than taking much risk by trading on their own behalf. The members of the Stock Exchange, for example, operated as a club and charged fixed commission fees for all clients irrespective of the size of business they were undertaking. This avoided competition between them, and enabled them all to survive without having to work too hard. The ready exchange of inside information and the use of insider trading, which was not heavily policed, meant that there were opportunities for further earnings, usually at the expense of outsiders. It was these features that enraged Mrs Thatcher when she took office, and this led eventually to the 'big bang' as a way of destroying this cosy insider oligopoly.

Corporate finance was focused on organising loans for companies engaged in restructuring or mergers and acquisitions. This classic 'merchant bank' function involved mobilising contacts and networks both to identify opportunities and to collect together underwriters and lenders. Again, the firms avoided risking much of their own capital. Other banks specialised in institutional investment, either on behalf of others such as company pension schemes, or through establishing their own unit trust or investment trust products for the retail market.

The City constituted a disparate group of small institutions mainly specialising in a particular set of transactions and activities. The 'big bang' reforms meant that it was now possible to merge these activities into one big financial institution, and this institution could have access to much more capital. Pulling these together created a much more enticing prospect in an era of shareholder-value capitalism, but it required a phase of reorganisation, consolidation and growth. So banks began to engage in a wider range of businesses.

First they expanded their lending activities by borrowing more themselves, not from retail depositors but from the wholesale financial markets, where big lenders – other banks, industrial firms, wealthy individuals and institutional investors – were looking to lend their money. The more that was borrowed and lent on to other borrowers, the higher a bank's profits and dividends for shareholders. But borrowers with strong credit ratings were already accounted for and did not need to borrow more. So banks had to encourage less credit-worthy individuals and institutions to borrow, notably in the subprime housing market.[5] This has some beneficial effects for the banks because they can charge higher interest rates, but it also increases the risk that borrowers will not be able to pay back.

In theory, the bank keeps reserves to protect against this, known as Tier 1 capital (that is, cash and other quickly realisable assets). But from the 1990s, these reserves shrank. One reason was that regulators developed 'smarter' reserve requirements by ranking assets in what was termed a 'risk-weighted' way and then setting reserve requirements according to risk. Banks themselves wanted to put less into reserves because these funds earned very little return, and from a shareholder value point of view were not being used effectively. Leverage ratios crept upwards.

Leverage refers to the proportion of Tier 1 capital in the total assets held on the bank's balance sheet. In banking terminology, *assets* usually refers to loans that the bank has made. If Tier 1 capital is set at 5 per cent of assets, then the leverage ratio is 20:1; if the Tier 1 capital is set at 3 per cent, then the leverage ratio is 33.3:1. The lower the Tier 1 capital, the more vulnerable the bank is to adverse conditions, as it has less cash in hand to pay out. In Lehman's case the leverage ratio was 31:1 by 2007. Despite regulators' concerns, reserves were shrinking at a time when risks were growing. Nevertheless so long as the market was moving upwards, shareholder returns kept rising. In effect the banks were borrowing more, increasing their leverage ratios – which was in itself a risk – but also borrowing more to lend on to subprime borrowers as well as to trade on their own account in the financial markets, further increasing risk.

If the wholesale markets began to be concerned that the banks which had borrowed funds could no longer pay them back because ultimately they were holding assets which were dependent on borrowers who were no longer able to sustain their repayments or were worth less than was previously thought, then the markets would either push interest rates up to those banks as short-term loans were renewed or refuse to renew them at all. This is what started to happen in 2007–08, culminating in the Lehman crash.

The 2000s saw a vast expansion in the range of markets in which these banks could trade: not just traditional stocks and bonds, though these remained important, but also what were known as over-the-counter (OTC) derivatives markets. Derivatives are essentially contracts in which actors agree to swap future risk. This could be currency risk (the largest market), interest rate risk or (more recently) credit risk, and there are also other more exotic forms of risk. These types of futures and options contracts had existed for a long time, but they had been mainly traded on regulated markets where the parties had to provide collateral. OTC markets were bilateral, and very little collateral was put up. They were low-margin but high-volume markets.[6] The risk was low if the parties hedged their bets by taking out protective contracts with others in the market, but this meant profit was low. So the temptation was increasingly not to hedge, not to provide collateral, but to take the high profits which shareholders liked, hoping that the risks proved as negligible as financial experts were claiming they were, and ignoring what Taleb described as the 'black swan' effect. This is that however improbable something seems, if it does come true, it shatters all previous expectations.[7] This was what happened in the financial crisis of 2008.

To encourage these ways of maximising shareholder value, senior managers in banks offered their managers, traders, dealers and advisers bonuses that rewarded high returns, without implementing an adequate risk measurement system. In proprietary trading as well as in the bond markets and OTC, losing a highly successful trader to a competitor was potentially disastrous, as the traders contributed so much to profitability. Internal compliance officers had a weak position compared with the dealers and traders. Traders were granted generous bonuses linked to the profits they made, but there was very little risk monitoring in terms of what these deals meant for the bank's overall financial position. The push was always to sell more, deal more, trade more and lend more. For dealers in trading rooms rewarded by huge bonuses and risking the bank's own money, the temptation was always to grow 'the book', to engage in more and more transactions and to look for ways in which hedging could be avoided. Similar pressures worked on dealers acting as intermediaries between the market and institutional investors. The more they could persuade their clients to buy and sell – known as 'churning' – the more fees they could generate. This also gave them opportunities to use their intermediary position to generate further profits by offloading their own stock onto clients at inflated rates.

Senior managers were rewarded on the performance of their bank as a whole. Their bonuses were therefore affected by the efforts of the traders and dealers, particularly since many other bank operations, such as retail services and lending to small and medium-sized enterprises (SMEs), were barely profitable. For the dealers there was limited downside to risk-taking but a huge upside reflected in their potential bonuses. The same went for their immediate managers and up the chain to the senior executives and directors. According to Robert Peston, top pay went up between ten and twenty times from 1990 to 2006. Fred Goodwin at RBS was paid just under £4 million in 2006 while Bob Diamond at Barclays Capital made £100.7 million. Even after the crash, in 2011 Diamond was paid £21 million.[8]

Shareholders too were happy with the situation so long as profits were being shown. In the end many of the dealers and managers lost their jobs as a result of the crash, but by no means all did so, and even those who did leave the business retained the huge bonuses they had received in the previous boom years, none of which have been returned.

At a simple level, therefore, the more money you had to work with, the more profit you could make even on very narrow spreads between buy and sell prices, even if you hedged your position by offsetting the risk. 'Normal' profits came from this arbitrage process, taking narrow margins on relatively risk-free deals. If you did not hedge, the risk became larger but the profit could become even greater. It is clear that many dealers did not hedge and as a result, whilst some became hugely successful, other spectacular cases emerged of dealers losing billions of pounds for their bank because they had held on to all the risk in the hope of gaining all the reward (see Box 7.1).

Nick Leeson at Barings Bank was an early example of this. In the early 1990s, he was able to keep his losses concealed for many months in the Singapore dealing room of the London-based bank while he continued to trade in the hope that he could regain his lost ground. He failed, and the bank collapsed. In 2008 Jerome Kerviel, a trader at the French bank Société Générale, was found to have lost €3.7 billion on the basis of unauthorised trades worth €49 billion – more than the capitalisation of the bank. Both went to prison for defrauding their employers and their clients.

It is common to label these individuals as 'rogue traders', yet the whole system was now built on these extreme types of trading activity, in order to maximise the benefit, for the traders individually, for senior executives and for shareholders. The ability of compliance officers to monitor these trading activities and in particular to discipline traders was limited. The models used to measure excessive risk in these situations were weak, ignored 'black swan' type risks and did not take into

---

Box 7.1 *The example of AIG: money for nothing*

AIG is a large US-based international insurance group. It set up a small office in the City of London which at the height of the financial boom began to enter into credit derivative swaps (CDSs). These were like an insurance against credit loss. So if Bank A lent Bank B £10 million and simultaneously entered into a CDS contract with AIG which involved it paying to AIG an annual premium each year for the length of the loan, then if Bank B failed to meet its credit obligations, AIG would become liable. A normal insurance contract of this sort would require that the insurer put aside a certain amount of the premium into its reserves to ensure that if the risk materialised it could pay the client. However CDS contracts were not insurance contracts; they were unregulated financial products, and there was no legal obligation on AIG UK to put aside any reserves or collateral. Even so, it might have been expected that a sensible management would make some provision for such an eventuality, but the management of AIG UK did not do so. Perhaps they felt that any losses would be minimal and could anyway be covered by the reserves of their parent company. They used the premiums to increase shareholder returns and to provide themselves with massive bonuses. Whatever the reason, they continued to sign contracts, guaranteeing to cover losses on lending. When the financial crisis came and debtors were declared in default, AIG's clients lined up demanding that AIG cover their losses. These demands rapidly put AIG itself into technical bankruptcy, and it had to be rescued by the Obama administration. This was only one of many examples where bankers and financiers took all the gains upfront without making anything like sufficient provision for losses once the markets changed. To prevent overall financial collapse, governments stepped in.[9]

---

account the possibility of simultaneous failures across multiple firms. All the impetus was on the trading side. Resistance, scepticism and alternative views were squeezed out of the system as regulators, politicians, shareholders, senior managers and traders engaged in a massive exercise in 'groupthink' and myopia. They saw nothing but benefits, and failed to take adequate account of the risks that were building in the system and in the individual firms, while pocketing the benefits of excessive risk taking.

Box 7.2 *Royal Bank of Scotland: making money from money and then losing it*

Under the leadership of Fred Goodwin, the Royal Bank of Scotland (RBS) had expanded rapidly in the early 2000s by borrowing heavily. With the funds which it borrowed it entered new markets, many of which turned against it in 2007–08. For 2007 and 2008 RBS made losses of £2.5 billion linked to structured credit, including CDOs in the US market. It had made a big push into this market in 2006 to gain shares in the subprime mortgage market, a disastrously bad decision launched at the worst possible time. Its corporate lending unit also grew rapidly, providing loans to businesses that were also subprime. Its forays into the commercial property market were also to prove disastrous, and to add further pain it purchased its rival ABN Amro at a very high price in 2007, when commentators were already warning that this was very bad value and that ABN Amro was very badly exposed to US subprime risk.

In October 2008 RBS had to be rescued by a £45 billion taxpayer bailout. Since then, RBS's weaknesses both before and after 2008 have been revealed. It was one of the worst offenders in selling personal customers payment protection insurance (PPI) that they did not need, leading to massive fines, huge repayments to customers and large administrative costs. In the wholesale markets, it has been identified as a major culprit in the effort to fix LIBOR rates, and in 2013 it was fined £390 million by regulatory authorities in the United States and the United Kingdom. The ramifications of the LIBOR scandal are not yet over, as this fixing resulted in many individuals and institutions losing money to the likes of RBS, and issues of compensation to the victims of this behaviour remain.

In-house regulators and those outside seem to have fought a losing battle to control the dealers and lenders, not least because as long as they were turning a profit for their bank, senior management, often unaware of how this was being achieved beyond naïve ideas of the business they were in, were happy for them to get on with it. Many commentators have also pointed to the 'moral hazard' involved. Banks felt they were too big to fail, and if they did get into trouble, governments and central banks would have no option but to rescue them. As it turned out this was correct, except that instead of a single bank being rescued behind closed doors by secretive actions by central bankers and the government, the simultaneous collapse of so many banks meant that everything was public and politicised. So the banks were actually 'too big to fail' and governments did rush to rescue them.[10]

Information Asymmetry: Keeping Clients in the Dark

Within their walls these market-dominating financial institutions had the full range of financial businesses: loans and bond issuance, investment management, corporate treasury management, financial advice on merger and acquisition deals, stock issuance, buying and selling stocks, bonds and other financial products for clients and for themselves in proprietary trading, currency trading, and swaps and derivatives trading on and off exchanges. By their scale and scope, they accumulated resources and information from all parts of the financial universe. Although regulators were supposed to ensure that there were 'Chinese walls' between various functions in order to avoid conflicts of interest, in fact such conflicts of interest were endemic. Information about a client, sector or bond issue that had a bearing on what was happening in other parts of the market could be accumulated and used by the bank to increase its profits.

There was huge information asymmetry between these institutions and the wider circle of medium-sized or specialist financial institutions with which they dealt.[11] Goldman Sachs even established something called an 'asymmetric service initiative', where its stock analysts briefed its traders on the advice they were going to give their clients, thus allowing the traders to move into the market first and take gains when clients started to act on the advice. Eventually the US SEC fined Goldman $22 million for indulging in this practice, as it was directly contrary to the Chinese walls that were supposed to eliminate any conflict of interest.

Banks arguably showed even worse behaviour when they advised clients to buy products which they knew were risky or worthless. In the dot-com boom, in the early 2000s, it emerged that analysts were promoting to their clients stock which they themselves thought was highly risky. Henry Blodget from Merrill Lynch notoriously rubbished stock that he cheerfully praised to clients who bought it at inflated prices. Blodget was banned from the securities industry and fined $2 million. As the housing boom of the mid-2000s developed, the structuring of bonds in complex ways and the efforts to promote them as risk-free because of the existence of 'credit default swaps' – a form of financial product which 'insured' a buyer of bonds against credit loss – became a central business in many investment banks. They sold these products to many clients who had little understanding of what was involved. Even when it became clear that there were increasing defaults amongst the mortgages on which these bonds were based, the banks continued to sell them to their clients.

Legal cases have forced institutions to admit to their culpability (after the event) and to pay fines and repay monies to their clients. In September 2013 a consortium of British banks – Barclays, Lloyds, HSBS and RBS amongst them – were fined for selling customers complicated derivatives they did not understand. Many more cases are being reviewed: the banks may have to consider over 30,000 cases of potentially mis-sold interest rate derivatives, including structured collars, swaps, simple collars and caps, otherwise known as interest rate hedging products.

Information asymmetry has enabled banks to play an even wider set of games in order to serve their own interests. Recent disclosure of how the LIBOR interest rate was manipulated is one example. In the financial crisis, bankers were desperate to ensure that their institution continued to be perceived as sound, so their treasury staff reported 'fictional' rates at which they would engage in overnight borrowing. In fact nobody was lending or borrowing at the height of the crisis, but to report this would have sent LIBOR rates sky high, with an impact on all LIBOR-related products, including most mortgages. As details of the LIBOR scandal leaked out, it became clear that this was not a one-off but that the rate had been continually manipulated over many years by the banks in order to suit their interests.

The central role of the big banks in shaping markets and prices, and thereby profitability, can also be seen in large initial public offerings (IPOs). The banks are brought in to advise on how to present the proposal to the public, including the price of the new shares. They underwrite the sales of the shares and use their client base to ensure that the shares are sold. In each of these processes, they accrue fees. They also accrue information, as they play a central role in setting the price of the shares. This is legitimated in terms of their knowledge of market demand and their skill in understanding the potential of the assets, but it leads to ambiguities and potential conflicts of interest. In cases where states are privatising some of their assets, it appears that prices are set deliberately low to ensure that all the shares are sold, so the underwriting fee is clear profit. These tactics have been the subject of significant debate in the United Kingdom in recent privatisations of state assets, as shown in Box 7.3.

> ### Box 7.3 *The Royal Mail sell-off: profiting from privatisations and IPOs*
>
> In 2013, shares in the privatised Royal Mail were sold initially at 330p, a price set by consultations between the government, Royal Mail, its financial advisers Lazards, and a consortium of banks underwriting the IPO. By the end of the first day of trading, shares had gone up to 489p, a tidy profit of 160p for those institutions and individuals who had received shares – and in theory a loss for the government and the taxpayer, as well as for the company itself, which could have used the extra funds to invest and develop. Instead the state had been effectively asset-stripped in the guise of privatisation. Meanwhile underwriters such as Goldman Sachs and UBS received over £12 million in fees for their role in what was a heavily over-subscribed issue, because of the general expectation that the shares were worth far more than 330p – an expectation which has proved correct, as they stayed over 500p into January 2014.
>
> As well as an inquiry by the Business, Innovation and Skills Select Committee, there have been reports on the Royal Mail sale from the National Audit Office (NAO) and the Public Accounts Committee. The NAO criticised the price at which shares were initially sold: 'The department was very keen to achieve its objective of selling Royal Mail, and was successful in getting the company listed on the FTSE 100. ... Its approach ... was marked by deep caution, the price of which was borne by the taxpayer.'[12] The City advisers had claimed that the offer might be under-subscribed, which was in part why they placed its price so low. As it was, the offer was 24 times oversubscribed. To make matters worse, in the light of their concerns that the offer would be under-subscribed, the government and the financial advisers had agreed to allocate many of the shares to 16 City-based institutions on the understanding that they would hold the shares for the long term. However, almost half of the shares allocated to them had been sold within a few weeks of the IPO.
>
> This manipulation of IPO prices to maximise benefits to City institutions at the expense of taxpayers reflects a raft of other privatisation IPOs going back to British Telecom in the Thatcher era, when the initial price was again set low, allowing quick profits to be made by banks and individuals at the expense of the taxpayer.

The Financial Outriders: Temptation and Collapse in Smaller Banks

Around the large financial institutions that effectively drove the system there were a range of other institutions. Two types of these had rather different consequences for the instabilities already described, but they operated similarly on the basis of 'light touch regulation' and a desperate desire to get in on the easy money that characterised the financial markets up to 2007.

First, there were banking institutions that were smaller in size, less sophisticated in terms of their understanding of the financial markets and the new products which were being developed, but which had dominant positions in their own contexts. Examples of this are banking institutions in countries such as Ireland, Iceland, Spain, Greece and Portugal, where politicians as well as bankers were seduced by the prospect of rapid growth which could be achieved through financial deregulation. If banks could borrow at relatively low interest rates from international financial markets, they could then lend these funds on in their own countries, most often sparking a property boom.

During the 2000s many countries had spectacular property booms thanks to the relaxation of credit. Rising house prices enabled home-owners to feel richer, and they could if they wanted remortgage to release some of the increased value of their house as money for consumption. Continued activity in the property market had many multiplier effects in retail, services and manufacturing, but it rested on an illusion that house prices would continue to rise while interest rates would remain low. In 2007–08, as these booms came to an end, individuals found themselves over-indebted, banks found their assets declining, and a general deceleration and reverse of the property market took place. There were consequent effects on employment, tax returns, social welfare payments and overall economic activity.

Second, similar illusions drew many smaller banking institutions (often former building societies) into believing they could become huge and powerful, and pay salaries to their senior executives to match their new size, simply by borrowing money from the wholesale markets and then lending it at a higher rate of interest to retail and business borrowers. Borrowers were tempted into this trap because the level of activity was pushing up asset prices: borrowing at the limit in year 1 would lead to a profit by year 3 because the price of the asset, mainly housing and commercial property, had climbed. Then the loan could be renegotiated or the property sold, and either way the borrower could take out some profit. The escalator of asset prices seemed to guarantee easy profits for the lender and the borrower – until the escalator stopped moving because asset prices were falling as individuals could no longer service their debts.

The demise of Northern Rock, summarised in Box 7.4, was merely the first example of non-City institutions both in the United Kingdom and overseas which were mesmerised by the opportunities opened up by easy borrowing to increase market share and boost earnings. These were not City slickers, more country cousins, but they could not resist the siren calls of easy money emanating from the City of London in the 2000s. Some were not even shareholder driven. The Co-operative Bank, which has no shareholders, only members, was tempted into these markets, in part because it bought another small financial institution, the former Britannia Building Society, which had turned itself into a bank and gone on a lending spree that eventually turned sour. Bank executives, not just in the United Kingdom but also in Ireland, Iceland, Denmark, Germany and many other counties, found it very difficult to resist the

---

Box 7.4 Ambition and disaster at Northern Rock

Northern Rock had been a traditional regional building society, but when it turned itself into a bank its ambitions grew. It borrowed from the wholesale markets and then lent this money on to a whole new group of customers. Northern Rock was one of the first to offer 100 per cent and more loans on mortgages; by the time it crashed it was even offering 125 per cent loan to value.

By 2007, it had borrowed £105 billion, most of it from short-term wholesale markets. It had to be able to renew these loans on a regular basis in order to sustain its high level of lending in long-term mortgage markets. By September 2007 there was no one willing to lend to it because its ability to meet its commitments was increasingly doubted, as housing prices stagnated and fell, and its borrowers began to fall behind on their payments. The Bank of England was approached to back up Northern Rock, but as this news went public, depositors who were concerned that their money would be lost started to descend on the bank to withdraw their funds. Soon bank branches and internet banking facilities were overwhelmed. Northern Rock could not be rescued; it had effectively to be taken over by the government and managed down in an orderly way.[13] In 2012, the rump of Northern Rock was sold to Virgin Money.

---

temptation of entering into the wholesale markets, to borrow short (cheap and easy) and lend long (risky and expensive). No doubt they were lured in by the high-pressure sales tactics of the large City-based institutions which promised to create gold from base metal, but their failure to see what was happening reveals the extent of the loss of moral compass and intellectual integrity which has pervaded the financial sector generally.

The ability of national states to rescue these second-tier institutions varied hugely, as did the path which they took to rescue. Ireland supported its banks by massive state loans in order to pay back creditors. It avoided high borrowing and instead slashed state expenditure. Iceland declared its banks bankrupt and refused to make their liabilities the responsibility of the state. This led to political pressure as well as a collapse of the Icelandic currency, with effects on living standards. In many of the Eurozone countries, states borrowed to support their banks until the point at which interest rates became prohibitive, leading to the ongoing crisis of the Eurozone in Greece, Portugal, Italy and Spain. The naïve belief of bankers and politicians that financial deregulation would lead to economic growth was repeated across many developed countries, which were running out of other options for growth as a result of the rise of the BRIC economies and the loss of manufacturing capacity. This explains the speed of contagion, through which the financial crisis was transmitted from London and New York to many other parts of the world.

The Shadow Banking System: Hedge Funds and Private Equity

The second group of outriders are those involved in the 'shadow banking' system, comprised of organisations that engage in lending and borrowing, and buying and selling, but with very little regulation. In an era when funds are tied to market indices and trading is increasingly on the basis of computer algorithms, making it relatively easy for anyone with the technology and expertise to match the market average in terms of returns, many wealthy investors look for alternative investments that could offer returns above the average. This is what hedge funds promise. They are activist funds, not passive index funds. This means that they search out risk but try to find ways to control the downside and maximise the upside, often through complex juggling and matching of different assets.

Hedge funds are in fact no more than large pots of money, originally sourced from very wealthy individuals but later also from institutional investors willing to gamble a small part of their total capital in the high-risk speculative activity which characterises this sector. Hedge funds are generally unregulated, though at the same time they do not enjoy the protection of central banks and governments. If they collapse, the investors lose their money. However the collapse of hedge funds can create a contagion risk for the rest of the financial system, because they will be counterparties in contracts with regulated banks, and their inability to pay their debts will therefore impact on the formal banking system. If institutional investors have placed capital with them which is lost, this will affect the balance sheet of the institutional investors, so the lack of regulation is a threat to the stability of the wider system.

Hedge funds are usually run by a small group of specialists who have developed an expertise on particular aspects of the markets. They use the money from their investors in all sorts of ways, but most of their activity takes place in the financial markets. Hedge funds have no interest in nurturing innovation or production. Their interest is entirely in prices in the financial markets, and in finding ways to benefit from the difference between buy and sell prices. Occasionally they engage directly with particular companies by taking shares and then forcing some restructuring or takeover that hikes the value of the shares – or alternatively short the shares and through other means try to push a company into collapse, as illustrated in Box 7.5.

Most hedge funds and their managers stay out of the limelight, engaging in highly technical and complex trading strategies that are rarely visible in the public domain. Usually the only visible results are the earnings of the hedge fund managers. Because the financial markets have become so complex, the price of any financial instrument can be materialised in multiple ways, whether it is a share or a bond, or wrapped in a derivative product of some sort, with various inscribed timelines in the future. Similarly any particular financial instrument can be linked in difficult-to-understand ways with another instrument, such as the link between interest rates in a country and its exchange rate with other currencies.

Hedge funds can develop complex models to understand these links and try to anticipate them in ways which enables the fund to move before the market and to take huge profits. There is no guarantee of success: formulas and algorithms, hunches and guesses may work at one time and completely fail at another, but when the market overall is rising, as it was up to 2007–08, the upward lift is likely to provide strong support to hedge funds. However, this can disappear when markets collapse as they did in 2008, and then retrench. In the aftermath many hedge funds did collapse, and the losses were absorbed either by individuals or by

---

Box 7.5 The Children's Fund (TCI):
active hedge funding on the stock market

TCI has a reputation for aggressive shareholder activism. It buys a small stake in firms and then tries to pressure managers to increase shareholder returns or face a TCI-led shareholder's revolt that may result in takeover or splitting up the firm. TCI was involved in the takeover of ABN Amro by RBS as well as in the Mittal Steel takeover of Arcelor. TCI is known for buying large stakes in flagging companies and forcing radical change. During one of its more bitter disputes, it ousted the chief executive of Deutsche Börse, Werner Seifert.

TCI is run in London by Chris Hohn. It pays some of its profits to a charitable foundation called the Children's Investment Fund Foundation. Hohn is estimated to be worth about £80 million though he has given away much more in charitable donations. One of Hohn's recent 'hedging' successes was with News Corp. After the phone-hacking scandal broke in 2011, News Corp's shares were in free fall. Against popular opinion, Hohn brought £500 million worth of shares, which are now worth £829 million, a 60 per cent increase.

---

the institutions which had lent to the hedge funds. Some hedge funds, however, had taken a contrarian position, betting that there would be a collapse in the market. They were able to take this position because others were prepared to sit on the other side of the debt. In the event, this small number of contrarians made massive profits.[14]

The structure of hedge funds also means that the managers can take a huge proportion of the profits for themselves. Small percentages of large funds can create annual returns to managers of many millions. Hedge funds therefore generally prefer anonymity – at least as regards the general public – as they do not want to be drawn into any discussion of justification. In this they are unlike bankers in public companies, who continue to profess their value to the wider community in spite of everything that has happened in the 2000s.

Occasionally the earnings of successful hedge fund managers, or their extravagant purchases of super-yachts, are revealed in the press. Some hedge fund managers thus became the most visible face of the vast riches that can be accumulated in the shadow banking sector. The richest hedge fund managers are in the United States, where people like Carl Icahn, John Paulson and George Soros are worth over £11 billion each. In *The Times* Rich List for 2013, the wealthiest hedge fund manager in the United Kingdom was named as Alan Howard of the Brevan Howard limited liability partnership: Howard was worth £1.5 billion in 2013 and was 48th on the Rich List.

Another major alternative investment option that grew dramatically in the 2000s was private equity. Private equity firms purchased core investments from large institutional investors. They then sought to invest these funds in buying existing companies, restructuring them in a variety of ways and then selling them back into the financial markets. A central part of the strategy was to borrow the bulk of the purchase price and then quickly sell off what were deemed as peripheral assets to the new business plan. As illustrated in Chapter 4, this could include selling off the land and buildings in which the purchased firm was located and then leasing them back, using this money to reduce borrowings. Earnings would also be used to pay off loans, thus restricting any room for further investment.

In the period of rising asset prices up to 2008, the private equity firm might only hold an asset for two years before it would be able to sell it back into the market, having reduced its borrowings so that much of the profit now went to the private equity firm and its investors. The general model was that the private equity firm took an annual fee of 2 per cent on the funds it was managing and then 20 per cent of the increased value of the asset. The result was that managers in private equity firms started to draw vast earnings, even greater than might be expected because these profits were taxed not as income but as investment earnings. In the period up to 2007–08 when borrowing was easy and asset prices rising, private equity could target the largest companies in the United Kingdom.

Companies could only defend themselves by convincing their shareholders that they could generate higher returns for them over the short and medium term than would result from selling out to private equity. The result was that the sheer presence of private equity pushed companies further down the shareholder-value maximisation route, discouraging investment and encouraging short-term measures of share buy-backs. The strategies pursued by private equity and by companies seeking to defend themselves against private equity pushed UK companies to reduce their investments further, to cut down on labour costs by shrinking their labour force or restructuring wages and conditions, and to find ways to outsource various services and activities.[15]

Private equity presented itself as a positive force capable of reorganising and reenergising firms on the basis of tightly focused managerial goals. Yet this was a myth. Private equity was very powerful in the mid-2000s because of its privileged tax position, the existence of low rates of interest that enabled it to borrow cheaply, a dynamic market for IPOs and restructurings, and finally the 'search for yield' amongst institutional investors that encouraged them to look for alternative assets. Once these conditions collapsed after the 2008 financial crisis, the growth in private equity investments also collapsed and the investors' ability to sell out within a few years for a quick profit disappeared. Private equity funds still exist, and they still control large swathes of industry, but they are no longer as aggressive towards quoted companies as they were in the mid-2000s.

What Can Be Done About These Practices

It is clear from these examples that the activities of major banks and other players in the financial markets have had no real economic value other than to produce financial gain for those involved. They have also had a destructive impact on many more worthwhile industrial and commercial enterprises. Some of the measures that are needed to eliminate the worst abuses and to create a more socially useful financial sector are:

- a structural reform of the banking sector to separate the traditional function of lending to businesses and individuals from the highly risky investment and trading activities
- effective controls on the bonus culture that has led to many of the major problems
- regulation and disclosure of the activities of hedge and private equity funds and other players in the shadow banking sector.

These measures are discussed in detail in Chapter 12.

Part II

The Reforms

8

A New Political Economy for the Corporation

The chapters in Part I highlighted some of the major abuses and problems that have emerged in the recent activities of large corporations. Part II is about what needs to be done about it. It requires a two-pronged attack on a corrupt, unfair and inefficient system. One part of this is about changes in current law and practice. The other is about the development and facilitation of more acceptable alternative forms of business organisation. Common to both is a different conception of the nature of large businesses as significant economic institutions. We call this a new corporate political economy, which is as much about a more realistic and politically acceptable vision of the corporate economy as it is about the formalities of company law.

The prevailing thinking and practice of corporate capitalism which has led to the abuses identified in Part I stems from a misconceived and counterproductive approach to political economy promoted by neoliberal economists and passively endorsed by lawyers. It is based on a number of apparently simple but highly contestable propositions:

- The first is that the underlying principle of corporate capitalism is the promotion and protection of shareholder value.
- This is related to the so-called agency theory, that company directors and managers are merely the agents of shareholders and therefore bound at all time to act in the interests of shareholders.
- A third limb of neoliberal theory is that a free and therefore efficient market in company shares will always in the end produce the optimum result.

As shown in earlier chapters, this model has been effectively promoted over the past 50 years, initially by Milton Friedman and his colleagues associated with the Chicago school of economics. It has been eagerly adopted and passed on to successive generations of corporate executives;

and it has been promulgated by business schools and widely implemented, especially in the Anglo-American sphere of influence.

As succeeding chapters will demonstrate, the propositions of this model prioritise short-term financial interests rather than longer-term corporate development. They also act to shift the attention of directors and chief executives from investment in and the development of their businesses, into an overriding focus on the price of their shares. It has encouraged takeover and merger activity which often is of greatest benefit to the investment banks and hedge funds who finance the deals and to the advisers – the lawyers and accountants – who draft the documents and manage the operations. This focus has diverted executives from serious and sustained consideration of their responsibilities to the wider societies in which they work – notably with regard to the payment of corporate tax and any resulting effect on public services such as health and education. By prioritising the interests of wealthy shareholders and financiers, the shareholder value model has contributed substantially to increasing inequalities in most developed economies. In the process the interests of employees and consumers and the importance of national economic stability or development have been sacrificed or marginalised.

Almost all of the propositions that underpin this neoliberal agenda are suspect – legally, pragmatically and morally.

In legal terms, the formal duties of directors have always been to promote the long-term interests of the company. This has been repeated time after time in the leading cases in common law jurisdictions. In one famous 19th-century case, the judges adopted the down-to-earth principle that 'there shall be no cakes and ale except those that are for the benefit of the company'.[1] This general principle was expanded and given statutory force in section 206 of the UK Companies Act 2006, which requires directors to 'act in a way that they consider in good faith would be likely to promote the success of the company for the benefit of its members as a whole'. In so doing they must have regard to the long-term consequences, the interests of employees, business relationships, impact on the community and the environment, reputation for high standards of business conduct and acting fairly between members. This list clearly identifies the wide range of interests and values that companies must serve, and directly dispels the myth that the duty of executives is to maximise the wealth of shareholders. If it were treated seriously, it would meet many of the concerns of the proponents of corporate social responsibility.

The law on the duties of directors also focuses on the long-term success of the company as such. In so doing it casts doubt on the agency theory that the company is in effect no more than the 'alter ego' of the shareholders acting collectively, and that the directors are merely their agents. The claim that only shareholders can have rights is equally misplaced. Again there is a long list of legal cases in which the courts have emphasised that directors are not bound to accept orders from their shareholders. And there is nothing in the general law of property that requires that any person or body of persons must be given absolute ownership and control of 'their property'. It is quite normal for control to be divided between different individuals or bodies – as in respect of matrimonial homes as between spouses, trust property as between the rights of trustees and beneficiaries, and some forms of common land between different classes of local residents. As will be seen, the division of property rights in this way is entirely appropriate for major corporate enterprises, and is much more in accord with the legal position than agency theory. And it has been shown to work effectively in Germany and other jurisdictions, where some specific decision-making powers are exercised by joint supervisory boards composed of representatives of both shareholders and employees.

In more practical terms, it seems obvious that the primary purpose and justification of a company is not to generate profit for shareholders but to produce goods or services that people want or need. In order for economic activity to get started or expand, however, it is often necessary to obtain an injection of capital. This can be provided in the form of loans, charged with interest and repayable in due course. Alternatively it can be raised in the form of debentures or loan stock, with a more or less fixed interest but often with priority over simple loans in the event of the failure of the business. Or it can, but need not, be raised as equity capital on which variable dividends are payable depending on the profitability of the enterprise, though this capital may be lost if the enterprise fails. Capital may be also be provided by members of a co-operative enterprise, in which the division between external investors and those directly involved as workers or suppliers or customers is minimised. All these forms of business are generally incorporated. And as incorporation is generally linked to limited liability, shareholders, members, directors and managers are none of them personally responsible for the debts and obligations of the company, which is treated as an entirely separate and independent legal entity.

Looked at in this rather limited way, the corporate form provides a convenient legal mechanism for the provision of capital for a wide variety of business enterprises, and it has been adopted in almost every jurisdiction throughout the world. It is attractive for both small businesses and larger enterprises, since it grants limited liability not only to share-holders but also to directors, managers and members of co-operatives. Although it is not a necessary or inevitable consequence of incorpora-tion, limited liability is now regarded as a key element of the standard corporate form.[2] It is generally justified as a way of encouraging the establishment and development of business enterprises which may not turn out to be profitable or sustainable, since investors or members of co-operatives would be reluctant to put all their personal assets at risk. But this arrangement means that neither investors nor managers – unlike partners in an unincorporated partnership – have an incentive to pay close attention to areas of risk, rather than sources of reward, as there is limited personal liability for failure. So although neither incorporation nor limited liability is inherently objectionable, their vulnerabilities as well as their merits must be borne in mind.

The problem for corporate political economy is that an approach to incorporation and limited liability that may be appropriate for small owner-controlled and financed companies in which the shareholders and directors are the same people, and in which they may reasonably claim that the company and its profit are their property, has been applied to much larger and more diverse corporate enterprises. This is exactly what the proponents of 'shareholder value' and 'agency theory' have done. Yet in these large enterprises there are many more significant stakeholders who can claim, and should be granted, some say in what is decided about the allocation of resources and the distribution of profits.

That is reflected, as has been seen, in section 206 of the UK Companies Act, which identifies the interests not just of shareholders but also of employees, of consumers and of those concerned about business standards and the environment as proper matters for directors to take into account. But more than that is required if the respective rights and interests of shareholders, managers, employees, consumers, governments and the population at large are to be recognised effectively. There has to be much greater flexibility and diversity in the ways in which rights of involvement in decision making and in the distribution of profit after re-investment are accepted and acted on. The successes of co-determination by shareholders and employees in Germany, of profit-sharing systems like those in the John Lewis Partnership, and of more traditional co-operative enterprises, described in Chapter 13, need to be more widely recognised, facilitated and developed by government action.

It must also be recognised that the problem of balancing the rights of shareholders with these other stakeholders has been exacerbated by developments in the nature of share ownership and the way in which shares are traded on the market. In the 1930s Berle and Means high-lighted the impact on the established conception of shareholding of the dispersal of share ownership.[3] Because it was difficult for the highly dispersed shareholders in a large corporation to exercise any effective managerial oversight, the relative power of directors and executives to manage their corporation in their own interests, instead of acting as stewards who balanced competing interests, was increasing, and there was a risk that it would be abused. It was assumed by some that this 'managerial revolution' was irreversible, and that state regulation would ensure its progressive fulfilment. Others argued that the powers and responsibilities of shareholders could be restored through action by the investment institutions and pension funds that emerged as major share-holders, or by shareholder activism. Neither of these expectations has proved to be accurate.

By the 1970s growth in the advanced capitalist economies was slack-ening, and the corporatist consensus became increasingly strained. This invited the neoliberal critique of the burdensome nanny state, and the associated celebration of lightly regulated markets, coupled with incen-tives in the form of reduced taxes for innovation and enterprise, and the development of new markets for financial products. The influence of agency theory on corporate governance has led to an increasing identifi-cation of senior executives with external shareholders through the use of stock options. In recent years, the development of active trading by fund managers who buy and sell shares on behalf of institutional investors and pension funds, and the emergence of wealthy hedge funds and sovereign wealth funds, along with the massive increase in the speed and volume of share trading, often guided by computerised algorithms, has exacerbated these trends. The resulting focus by managers on short-term share price movements rather than longer-term investment has been identified by a series of official and independent reports as a serious problem.[4]

These developments in share ownership and market trading point to a further less legal but more significant aspect of the nature of major national and multinational enterprises that employ thousands of people and raise capital in highly complex ways. The proper way to look at these huge enterprises, as Veblen and more modern social organisation theorists have argued, is as socio-economic institutions in their own right.[5] Over time they may develop independently, they may merge or marry with others, and they may survive for lengthy periods before they decline and die. As such they have a life of their own and cannot sensibly be treated as little more than the property or agents of their shareholders. As productive social institutions they should be encouraged to invest in more socially and environmentally acceptable modes of operation, and they should be allowed reasonable forms of protection from self-interested manipulation either by dominant shareholders or hedge funds seeking short-term gains in market trading or in arbitrage during takeover bids. This too should be recognised and reflected in the legal regime under which they operate. The ways in which these problems can be dealt with are set out in Chapter 11.

From a broader societal perspective, reforms of this kind could help to reduce the divisive impact of the capitalist system. In his account of the economic effects of capitalism, Thomas Piketty has argued that capital left unregulated can lead to increasing inequality and social tensions between the haves and the have-nots, as in the decades before 1914 and since the 1970s; but also that with effective political regulation and taxation, as in the period from the 1930s to the 1970s, it can contribute to increasing equality and stability.[6] Piketty's proposed remedy is a progressive wealth tax, but his analysis is weak on the role of corporations, other than some comments on the recent escalation of the earnings of top corporate executives. The real significance of his analysis for corporate reform is that it shows that political action to ensure that the benefits of capitalist enterprise are more equally shared can have significant positive impacts on social cohesion.

What is needed, for all these reasons, is a reformulation of the political economy of major corporations that is a better reflection of the realities of the way in which they operate as social institutions, and of the legitimate interests of all the stakeholders involved or affected by their operations. As will be argued in the chapters that follow, this will require action on a number of related fronts:

- the recognition of the corporation itself as a significant 'actor' and institution that is vulnerable, and therefore merits protection from the vagaries of shareholder and market manipulation
- strengthening the rule that directors must look to the long-term interests of the company and dispelling the mythology of 'shareholder value'
- the development of more effective and balanced governance structures that provide appropriate levels of involvement in major decisions not only by shareholders but also by other parties, such as employees, suppliers and consumers
- the provision of structures for profit sharing in more equitable and effective forms than the (passive) distribution of shares to employees.

9

Controls on Multinationals

The dominant position of major multinational corporations throughout the world is well established. That cannot be denied or changed. What can be done is to develop more effective regulation of the way in which they operate to prevent the wide range of abuses that have been documented and illustrated in the earlier chapters. This chapter sets out a strategy for dealing with the major problems.

The most immediate concern is the way in which multinationals have been allowed to develop complex corporate structures in different jurisdictions that have enabled them to avoid paying the tax that other smaller and nationally based companies have had to pay. The behaviour of many leading multinationals in seeking and usually succeeding in minimising their tax liabilities by locating aspects of their operations in tax havens, often by spurious claims about the real location of decision making, is clearly abusive and contrary to any conception of corporate social responsibility. It gives them an unfair competitive advantage over nationally based competitors.

In more general terms the financial and political power of major multinationals and their ability to relocate their operations gives them individually and collectively the opportunity to drive down levels of taxation, payments for mining and other extraction rights, and other forms of regulation, and thus to shift and externalise the social and environmental costs of their operations. The result is to add to and entrench the economic imbalance between richer Western and poorer developing economies. By extracting value from poorer to richer economies in this way, multinationals are major contributors to the unfair trading relationships that the international community finds it so difficult to alter.

A related concern is the difficulty that national governments, competitors, employees and other outsiders face in establishing accurate and realistic accounts for the subsidiaries or divisions of multinationals operating within their jurisdictions. The lack of clarity on true levels of profitability and stability gives these externally controlled enterprises a negotiating advantage in their dealings with national and local governments, trade unions and other parties in discussions over incentives for foreign direct investment and over levels of pay for employees. Ultimately they can wield the threat of relocation. As in most other spheres of business, control over the flow and the content of financial information is a crucial factor in all these matters.

A further somewhat different concern is the ability of foreign-controlled enterprises to avoid full liability for disasters and debts resulting from their local operations. This stems mainly from the limited liability enjoyed by locally incorporated subsidiaries, and the difficulty in establishing or enforcing liabilities up the corporate chain, though a similar result can be obtained managing the supply chain. By contracting or subcontracting production to locally owned enterprises, as in respect of clothing and other similar products which are in practice controlled and managed by foreign purchasing companies, the externally managed companies can effectively shift their risks and responsibilities to others. The recent disasters resulting from unregulated and jerry-built factory premises in Bangladesh, as set out in Chapter 4, are only the most well-publicised examples of this form of avoidance.

Understanding Corporate Complexity

The underlying legal problem is the freedom of multinationals – and large national corporate groups – to create complex corporate structures that permit them to organise and portray their affairs for maximum financial and political advantage.[1] This is typically done by establishing a complex web of subsidiaries and associated companies in different jurisdictions, which enables multinationals to assert or pretend that different aspects of their operations are owned and controlled in those jurisdictions – actual production and research and development in one or more places, corporate banking and financial operations in others, profitable trademarks and royalty income in tax havens, and so-called 'management services' – the payment for senior executives – wherever executives can pay the least personal tax. In reality, however, the whole operation is managed and directed from group headquarters, typically on a more functional and rational basis, with a number of separate divisions cutting across the national corporate structures and giving authority to divisional executives to issue instructions to managers of linked operations throughout the world.

In formal terms, however, highly complex corporate structures are almost always preserved and developed. It is well known, both from their formal annual reports and accounts and from more detailed individual studies, that most large multinationals have very large numbers of subsid-iaries, often numbered in the hundreds.[2] Most of these are wholly owned and have been acquired as a result of takeovers and mergers or the need to create operating or trading subsidiaries in each of the many jurisdictions in which they carry out business. Many multinationals have in addition entered into joint ventures with other companies or have inherited other partly owned or associated companies. Further complexity often results from the deliberate creation of a range of special-purpose subsidiaries or associated companies within the group. A kind of internal corporate bank is often established in a tax-efficient jurisdiction to handle the flow of internal loans and deposits that group finance directors require in the interests of overall group financial management. Other subsidiaries or formally uncontrolled associated companies may be established to facilitate less obviously legitimate operations, such as off-balance-sheet financing or tax avoidance. And where these are located in jurisdictions in which annual accounts are not publicly available, there is an addi-tional concern that the objective may be to conceal the true nature or effect of the transactions involved. The sheer complexity of the resulting legal structures certainly increases the difficulty that outsiders face in unravelling the underlying managerial and financial realities.

All this cuts across the legal fiction that all of the incorporated companies in the group are formally and legally separate, each with its own board of directors and its own financial statements and obliga-tions. It also results in the systematic neglect or disregard of the formal rules of company law in most jurisdictions. A centralised group banking system through which surplus funds in one company are reallocated to support or develop the business of another, often without the payment of even notional interest, is a denial of the fundamental rule that the directors of each company are required to act only in the interests of their own company. This is in any case fundamentally undermined by the fact that any director or executive at lower levels within the group can be dismissed if they do not comply with instructions from group head-quarters. A formal power to remove directors by fax or email is regularly inserted into the articles of association of subsidiary companies. And where the real business of the group is organised – and also accounted for at group level – in non-corporate divisions, the production of indi-vidual annual accounts for each subsidiary can become a more or less meaningless accounting chore.

This disconnection between formal corporate structures and the realities of multinational management practice has important impli-cations for accounting and taxation. A telling recent development in international accounting rules is the introduction of a requirement that data on the segments of business operations should be reported in such a way that the information in group accounts will correspond with the way in which those segments are actually managed.[3] However, there is continuing concern over the variability in the way in which this has been interpreted. There is a continuing lack of clarity on how the audited accounts of individual subsidiaries or sub-groups are related to these segmental or divisional results.

There is a similar lack of clarity, as explained further in Chapter 10, on how the figures for taxation in annual group or individual company accounts relate to tax that is eventually paid. In many jurisdictions the accounts submitted for taxation purposes differ from those published in annual company reports, and there follows a negotiation with the tax authorities over the basis on which tax is to be assessed. As this usually takes several years, the figures for tax in annual accounts are provisional and may change substantially when a final assessment is made. To deal with this there is a further accounting standard, *FASB Interpretation 48 on Accounting for Uncertainty in Income Tax*, designed to govern the way in which this uncertainty is reported.[4] This prescribes a 'more likely than not' standard for the statement of tax liabilities in annual published accounts, but that is determined by the company and its auditors, and may differ substantially from what is finally agreed with the tax authorities. All this again creates difficulties in establishing what tax is payable or paid on the results of individual businesses operations within a multinational group.

There is an equally worrying disconnection in respect of corporate decision making. The formal legal position, as already indicated, is that the legal responsibility for what is decided and carried out lies with each individual company and its directors within the multinational group. In practice the major decisions on policy and investment are made at group headquarters, and executives in subsidiaries are expected to carry out instructions from their divisional managers. Whether they are appointed as directors or not is more a matter of prestige and status than real power or effective responsibility, and in the largest and most complex multinationals this can and often does result in serious problems. Demands to achieve financial targets imposed by group executives are likely to take precedence over concerns about the impact on employees, local communities or the environment at local levels. The flow of information on these concerns from operating plants or subsidiaries up the chain of command is inevitably affected by what are perceived to be priorities at group level. There is a growing realisation that some of these complex group enterprises are simply 'too big to manage'.

This disconnection between management systems and legal structures creates major difficulties for any attempt to regulate or control the way in which major multinationals behave. The freedom and flexibility they enjoy to structure their legal forms as they wish gives them a huge competitive advantage over both governments and their national competitors, in that they can organise or reorganise themselves to avoid or evade many well-intentioned tax or regulatory provisions.

The Objectives of Regulation

The objectives of regulation must be to curtail this freedom and flexibility and to impose a legal regime on multinationals that is a better reflection of the way in which they actually operate. This will not be easy to achieve, given both the power of multinationals to lobby against any proposals that might affect their profitability, and the continuing competition between national governments to persuade major foreign companies to invest and locate their operations in their countries. It will necessarily involve agreement and action both at an international level, and also some requirements and coordination for national legislation. This has already been accepted, as will be seen in Chapter 10, within the OECD in respect of taxation. It has also been adopted more generally within the United Nations in the *Guiding Principles on Business and Human Rights*[5] in respect of the responsibilities and obligations of businesses to protect human rights. These provide a useful focus on the interrelationship between the obligations of multinationals to comply with broader international standards and the duties of national governments to adopt legislation and monitoring systems to ensure that they do so.

This most recent attempt to deal with human rights and related abuses by multinationals within the United Nations began with a draft set of *Norms on the Responsibilities of Transnational Corporations and other Business Enterprises with regard to Human Rights* developed by the Sub-Commission on Human Rights in 2003. These sought to impose general human rights obligations not only on states but also directly on multinational corporations, which were to be obliged to adopt codes of conduct on human rights and to report on their implementation in some unspecified manner. But there was concerted opposition to this draft from some developed states and their multinationals, and no further progress was made. Instead a Special Representative of the Secretary-

General, John Roggie, was appointed to work on an alternative approach. His proposal for a tripartite 'protect, respect and remedy' formulation in 2008 was received more favourably, perhaps because it focused on the primary responsibility of individual states to adopt measures to deal with and provide remedies for human rights abuses by companies within their jurisdictions. Within this framework multinational corporations would be expected only to develop internal codes of conduct to respect the full range of internationally agreed human rights standards. Roggie's more detailed *Guiding Principles on Business and Human Rights*, endorsed by the Human Rights Council in 2011, follow this model closely, and for the moment remain in the realm of 'soft law' which is not actually binding on either states or multinationals.

Given the difficulty at an international level in attempting to impose enforceable obligations on private-sector companies, the most promising strategy may be to encourage individual states to adopt national laws to that effect, as envisaged in the Roggie framework. As will be seen, however, the weakness of the *Guiding Principles* and other codes of conduct, such as the *OECD Guidelines for Multinational Enterprises,* is the lack of focus on the complexity of multinational corporate structures, linked to the absence of any effective provisions for monitoring or enforcement.

So more needs to be done if a more acceptable and effectively responsible form of international capitalism is to be achieved.[6] That will require the building of strategic alliances by activists to put pressure on an incoming UK government, on other concerned governments and on international bodies, to agree a number of strategic objectives and work towards the implementation of the necessary measures.

The underlying objectives of this coordinated international and national approach should be focused on four issues: the simplification of formal corporate structures; the development of country-by-country reporting as the basis of fair and effective corporate taxation; the localisation of reporting, decision making and responsibility for compliance with national legislation and human and environmental rights conventions; and ultimate group liability to ensure that this is achieved effectively. The essential basis of all the elements of these strategic objectives is an increase in transparency and clarity of responsibility.

Simplification of corporate structures will require action at group level. This can best be approached through stock exchange requirements for major quoted companies: the listing requirements for major multinational corporations already impose detailed reporting and governance requirements at group level, and could introduce similar requirements in respect of more straightforward and transparent legal structures. This would be easier to achieve and enforce as an international listing requirement than by national legislation.

Country-by-country reporting is essential both for taxation, as discussed in Chapter 10, and for the implementing and monitoring of international standards on a wide range of environmental and labour standards issues. That will require international action both as a condition of listing and at a national level in respect of the preparation and publication of country reports.

Localisation of reporting and decision making is designed to ensure that actual operations in each jurisdiction/country are recorded and reported on a true and fair basis. This is clearly required for the OECD approach to taxation. There is also a need for greater authority in the boards of directors in each jurisdiction to assert their independence on compliance with national legislation and standards of conduct, and to report and publicise unlawful or inappropriate instructions from group headquarters. An effective element of national governance is mandated by the *UN Guiding Principles*.

Unitary responsibility must be focused on imposing ultimate financial responsibility on the holding company for debts and torts by subsidiaries and associated companies where effective control is exercised by the holding company. In some circumstances this should be extended to elements in the supply chain, notably in clothing and similar manufacturing contracts where there is dominant control over the low-cost supplier.

Simplifying Corporate Structures

The underlying objective is to require major multinationals to adopt corporate structures that reflect the reality of their operations, just as their segmental accounts are already required to correspond to 'the way in which management organises segments within the enterprise for making operating decisions and assessing performance'. As has been stressed in other chapters, incorporation is a privilege and should not be allowed to be used in such a way as to obfuscate or conceal the true and fair state of affairs within major multinational groups. A significant contribution to this could be made at national level by a requirement for the incorporation of a single holding company for all group enterprises with a significant presence within the jurisdiction. That would provide a practical legal basis for monitoring and enforcement action. It is impractical, however, to rely on national legislation for the simplification of the overall structure of multinational groups. A more effective strategy would be to require major multinational groups whose shares are traded on international stock exchanges to adopt prescribed legal structures as a condition of listing. This could readily be argued for and justified as an important step towards the transparency that even the most market-oriented national and international authorities purport to require. It would also allow a degree of flexibility through the established mechanisms for the approval of listings that might not be so easily achieved under a more formal legislative regime.

Country-by-Country Transparency

All forms of group accounting and disclosure by major quoted multinational are tightly regulated by international accounting standards and enforced by listing rules on the major stock exchanges. Currently these rules focus almost exclusively on the content of annual and interim reports, including overall group accounts, payments of group directors and executives, lists of operating subsidiaries and associated companies, and what are termed segmental results. The accounting standards on group accounts are not entirely satisfactory. They fail to give satisfactory details of estimated and eventually assessed tax for each jurisdiction, as discussed in Chapter 1, of the internal transfers and loans within the group, or of potential risks to accounting for each subsidiary on a going-concern basis. More revealing procedures on most of these have been developed and proposed by academic accounting experts, notably in Sydney.[7]

The most directly relevant aspect of this, however, is that fact that many of these accounting rules cut across the formal legal corporate structures of the group, for example in respect of segmental accounts. If groups can be required to ignore long-established corporate structures for this purpose, there is no compelling reason that they should not be required to do so for other purposes, such as the simplification of those structures and the abandonment of more or less fictitious incorporations in tax havens or jurisdictions in which peculiar transactions can be concealed from public view.

A requirement for country-by-country reporting is already under consideration in respect of the new taxation systems under development within the OECD, discussed in detail in Chapter 10. It is also implied as one of the obligations for major business enterprises under Principle

21 of the *UN Guiding Principles*, which states that 'in order to account for how they address their human rights impacts, business enterprises should be prepared to communicate this externally, particularly when concerns are raised by or on behalf of affected stakeholders'. This and the associated commentary suggest that there should be direct and accessible communication with those most affected, but it is less clear how this should be done, and by what body the communication should be made. Linking these and other country reporting requirements, either to a country-based holding company or as a condition of the registration of business enterprises operating within a jurisdiction, as is required in many legal systems, would be a relatively simple means of implementation.

Localisation of Decision Making

All the established international codes of conduct for multinationals, including the *OECD Guidelines for Multinational Enterprises* and the *UN Guiding Principles,* emphasise the obligation on foreign-based or controlled businesses to comply with local laws. The most recent version of the *OECD Guidelines,* revised in 2010, focuses on the obligation of multinationals operating outside their home state to comply with local law, to contribute to local development, to protect human and environmental rights, and to abstain from any form of bribery or corruption. The equivalent provision of the *UN Guiding Principles* is that:

> in all contexts business enterprises should (a) comply with all applicable laws and respect internationally recognised human rights, wherever they operate; (b) seek ways to honour the principles of internationally recognised human rights when faced with conflicting requirements; (c) treat the risk of causing or contributing to gross human rights abuses as a legal compliance issues wherever they operate.
>
> (Principle 23)

The difficulty is that it is not always clear where the effective responsibility for compliance is located. The *OECD Guidelines* treat multinational enterprises as if they were a single entity with effective control over all their operations. The *UN Guiding Principles* also stress the obligation to adopt commitments 'at the most senior level of the business enterprise' (Principle 16), and the recommendations for carrying out due diligence (Principle 17) and impact assessments (Principle 18) only refer to assigning responsibility 'to the appropriate level and function within the business enterprise' (Principle 19). The reality in many complex and widely dispersed multinational groups is that while appropriate paper commitments are usually made at group level, there is less clarity on the responsibilities and powers of directors and executives in subsidiaries and joint ventures lower down the chain. The directors and executives at group level do not and probably cannot know what is going on at every level, and lower-level directors and executives are likely to be cautious about raising difficulties in the implementation of group financial strategies and targets.

There should be specific measures to enable directors and executives within multinational corporations to raise and publicise concerns as 'whistleblowers' without jeopardising their positions. A specific obligation on national subsidiaries and ultimate holding companies to investigate and report on such concerns, and/or for other stakeholders to call for special audits, as proposed in Chapter 11, should also be included.

Joint and Unitary Responsibility

The final essential element in this context must be an enforceable obligation on ultimate holding companies to compensate all those affected by unlawful conduct in other jurisdictions by their subsidiaries, associated companies and closely directed suppliers. This will require a more concerted and effective approach to the long-standing legal principle of the separate corporate identity and independence of each incorporated company.

In traditional company law terms this has been accepted as a fundamental principle, and measures to 'pierce the corporate veil' to impose liability on those who control the company, whether as individuals or via holding companies, have been of limited and uncertain effect. The approach of most judges, particularly in cases involving very large amounts of money, has been to maintain the legal fiction that each company within a group must be regarded as a formally and financially distinct entity, leaving it to those affected to use other means to persuade holding companies to meet their liabilities.

Some attempts have been made in the United Kingdom and other common law jurisdictions to provide a clearer and more predictable set of rules for group liability. The UK Companies Act has introduced the concept of liability for shadow directors in accordance with whose wishes the affairs of a company are managed, and it has been argued that this would normally apply within centrally managed groups and would thus result in effective group liability. In Australia a slightly different approach has been adopted, under which centrally managed groups can opt to accept full group liability but in return are absolved from producing annual accounts for subsidiaries for which they accept liability.[8] However this reduces still further the ability of stakeholders in substantial operating subsidiaries to obtain any information on the profitability or solvency of the enterprise they are dealing with.

In the United States, as outlined in Chapter 4, there has until recently been greater interest in the impact of a long-forgotten law, the Alien Torts Act of 1789, introduced to deal with piracy. Protracted litigation in US courts in respect of serious human rights abuses by some leading multinationals in developing countries has led to substantial voluntary settlements, and raised expectations that more general group liability for all foreign abuses might become established. However, the final Supreme Court decision in *Kiobel* v *Royal Dutch Petroleum*, in respect of alleged complicity by Shell in murder and looting by agents of the Nigerian government in the oil-producing Niger delta, has cast doubt on this as an effective remedy.

A better approach on this issue has been developed in Germany in a well-established set of rules known as *Konzernrecht* in respect of group liability.[9] This creates a number of distinct regimes for different forms of group structure and management. In particular it imposes full group liability in respect of subsidiaries which are managed on an integrated basis, under which the holding company can impose decisions on subsidiaries which would otherwise not be in the interests of the subsidiary as an independent company. In other cases the holding company is required to compensate the subsidiary or associated company for any loss it may have suffered as a result of group operations.

This set of laws is closely associated with German tax regimes, and is not entirely satisfactory as a general model for other countries. But the underlying concept that in centrally managed financially integrated groups of companies the ultimate holding company should in principle be responsible for all its activities in all jurisdictions is sound, and should be pursued as the basis for more general company law reform. And unlike in Australia this should not be adopted as an optional regime linked to an exemption from the publication of financial results on the performance of major operating subsidiaries. The basis of legislation should rather be that full group liability for wholly owned and controlled subsidiaries should be treated as the normal regime, and that where this is arguably inappropriate for specific enterprises or joint ventures, the separate identity and fully independent management of the exempted company should be publicly revealed and made enforceable by the full range of stakeholders, as in any other independent company or group.

How It Can Be Done

These controls can be developed by a combination of international taxation, stock listing, accounting and reporting regulations:

- There is already active engagement at an international level on the elimination of tax avoidance and evasion by multinationals as explained in Chapter 10. This approach needs to be expanded into other areas.
- The most effective means of simplifying corporate structures and increasing transparency is through national action on the listing rules in the main stock exchanges in which the shares of multinationals are traded.
- The imposition of effective measures on the localisation of decision making will require coordinated action at national level to develop systems of governance that reflect the full range of stakeholders in each jurisdiction, as discussed in Chapter 11.

An appropriate starting point on all these issues is the development of a framework convention which would allow individual states some flexibility in introducing national legislation.[10] The role for the UK should be to give a lead in developing its national legislation on transparency, governance and stock trading, and in promoting international action not only on fairness in taxation but on other development, environmental and human rights issues.

Controlling International Tax Avoidance and Evasion

The state fiscal crises which followed the financial crash of 2007–09 focused heightened political attention on tax evasion and avoidance. Austerity policies pursued by many governments were contested by movements such as Uncut, linking up with a worldwide tax justice movement which had grown in the previous decade. This focused on the importance of tax revenues, not only to fund collective public services, but also as a key element in moving poorer countries away from dependence on aid and towards sustainable development and democratic accountability.[1]

In response to these pressures, world leaders have called for reforms to the international tax system. There has finally been a long-overdue recognition of the major defects in this system, both resulting from and caused by the decades of systematic tax avoidance by multinationals. As discussed in Chapter 1, multinationals have abused the freedom to create complex corporate group structures to exploit the flaws in international tax rules based on the separate entity/arm's length principle (SE-ALP). However, the reform efforts so far have aimed only to patch up the system, without repairing these basic flaws. Only continued determined political pressure has forced political leaders and the technocrats in charge of the system to begin to move towards effective changes.

The reforms have focused on two main areas: corporate and tax transparency, and international corporate tax rules. These are discussed in the next two sections, while the third section puts forward proposals for more radical reforms.

Transparency

Growing concern in the 1990s about tax havens and offshore secrecy led to an initiative launched by the then G7 world leaders in 1996. The tax aspects were referred to the OECD's Committee on Fiscal Affairs (CFA). This resulted in the OECD's report in 1998 on *Harmful Tax Competition: An Emerging Issue*.

This project was effectively derailed by a change in US policy, when the new Bush administration accepted arguments that the initiative entailed dictating tax policy to other states, and that tax competition should be considered good. The project then refocused on obtaining information from tax havens, pursued at first through negotiation of bilateral tax information exchange agreements (TIEAs). To monitor this process the OECD set up a Global Forum on Transparency and Exchange of Information for Tax Purposes, which included the tax haven jurisdictions, so assembling a gang of foxes to guard the hen coop. This approach was criticised by the Tax Justice Network (TJN) from its foundation in 2003, which argued for a multilateral framework including automatic exchange of information as well as on request.

TJN also continually stressed the need for all states to introduce effective measures of corporate transparency for tax enforcement purposes, such as registers of ownership, without which there can be little information to exchange about tax evaders. Jurisdictions such as the British Virgin Islands are well known as easy places to form shell companies behind a veil of secrecy, since there are no ownership registers. Yet in practice leading countries such as the United States and the United Kingdom have also been among the main secrecy jurisdictions. In the United States company formation comes under state law. A report in 2006 by the US Government Accountability Office showed that none of the states require ownership information to be filed on company formation, and for the few that do require such information subsequently, it is not part of the public record. This makes the United States, especially the state of Delaware, an easy place to form shell companies to conceal all kinds of activities.[2] Studies have shown that company registration agents are more willing to turn a blind eye to 'know your client' rules in the leading financial centres such as the United Kingdom and the United States than in jurisdictions usually thought of as tax havens.[3]

Although both the United States and the United Kingdom have introduced obligations for banks and other paying agents to supply information on payments made to their taxpayers, these obligations do not cover taxpayers of other countries, who are therefore able to open accounts in London and New York protected by bank confidentiality. In 2003 the European Union introduced the Savings Directive, requiring banks throughout the Union to supply information on recipients of interest payments.[4] Eventually, in 2009 the US Congress introduced more stringent reporting requirements in the Foreign Account Tax Compliance Act (FATCA). Although this applies even to non-US banks if they have US clients, it still did not extend to non-US taxpayers. However, when the US authorities began negotiating agreements with other states to help enforce FATCA, some asked for reciprocity, so the net began to be widened. Gradually bank account reporting requirements have become multilateralised. However, it is still possible to use a shell company to conceal beneficial ownership of a bank account or other assets. Hence, company transparency obligations remain crucial.

The task of establishing systems for the new tax transparency standard is now being pursued by the OECD. A significant step was already taken in 2010, when the multilateral Convention on Mutual Administrative Assistance in Tax Matters, developed jointly by the Council of Europe and the OECD, was thrown open to all states, and the OECD began to encourage all states to join. Membership can be particularly helpful to developing countries, since it establishes a basis for exchange of information on request without the need for a bilateral double tax treaty. Automatic exchange of information (AEOI) is also provided for in that convention, although it requires a supplementary agreement to establish procedures.

Only after a further decade or more of campaigning have world leaders finally made a commitment at the 2013 G8 summit meeting to establish a new global standard of multilateral and automatic exchange of tax information, as well as transparency of beneficial ownership of companies and other entities:

> We commit to establish the automatic exchange of information between tax authorities as the new global standard, and will work with the Organisation for Economic Cooperation and Development (OECD) to develop rapidly a multilateral model which will make it easier for Governments to find and punish tax evaders. ... We agree to publish national Action Plans to make information on who really owns and profits from companies and trusts available to tax collection and law enforcement agencies, for example through central registries of company beneficial ownership.[5]

At this stage, these are only voluntary national commitments to establish registers of beneficial ownership of companies and other vehicles. Achieving practical and effective systems will certainly be an arduous and lengthy process. At the request of the G20 the OECD has prepared a common reporting model, including a Model Competent Authority Agreement, which was approved by the G20 Finance Ministers and Central Bank Governors' meeting in February 2014. Implementation of this template will be supervised by the Global Forum on Transparency and Exchange of Information for Tax Purposes, which has established a Group on AEOI. However, there is no formal requirement to join the Global Forum in order to adhere to the multilateral assistance convention, although doing so would facilitate negotiation of the agreements necessary to activate AEOI.

TJN has also campaigned for country-by-country reporting (CbCR), to require multinationals to produce reports covering the whole corporate group, including details of tax due and taxes actually paid in each country.[6] Although this was resisted by the International Accounting Standards Board, determined campaigning, especially through the Publish What You Pay coalition, succeeded in achieving some national and regional laws for CbCR.[7] The Extractive Industries Transparency Initiative (EITI) has established a global standard for disclosure of company payments and government receipts, governed by a multi-stakeholder model.[8] This has now inspired formal legal requirements in the United States and the European Union. The Dodd–Frank Act[9] introduced an obligation for any company subject to SEC filing to report on a country-by-country basis any payments made to government or public agencies in connection with development of oil, gas or mineral reserves, by project and business segment.

A similar requirement was enacted in July 2013 by the European Union for reporting, for financial years after 2016, by companies formed in the European Union involved in oil, gas, minerals or logging of natural forests, of payments made to each government and per project.[10] The European Union's Fourth Capital Requirements Directive, also passed in 2013, requires national legislation for all credit institutions (including banks) and investment firms to report for each company on its activities, turnover, employees, profit/loss before tax, tax paid on profit, and public subsidies received.

These specific sectoral provisions for CbCR have now been extended by the mandate from the G20 for the CFA to develop a global template for corporate reporting for tax purposes, as part of the project to combat Base Erosion and Profit Shifting (discussed in the next section). A significant difference is that the specific sectoral regulations require public disclosure, whereas the OECD appears to envision disclosure only to tax authorities.

The requirement for CbCR for tax purposes could transform international corporate taxation. The reporting template should include consolidated accounts of corporate groups as a whole, as well as country-by-country data on profits, employees, sales, and taxes due and paid.

If this can be made effective it would help to reveal whether in fact multinationals are being taxed 'where economic activities take place and value is created', as the G20 has mandated and discussed further below. The progress made so far on this is the result of sustained and well-informed political campaigning, the continuation of which remains vital to secure successful implementation.

Patching Up International Tax Rules

The renewed political pressures resulting from the fiscal crisis finally led the G20 world leaders in July 2012 to press for action through the CFA, which set up a project on Base Erosion and Profit Shifting (BEPS). After a year's work, this produced an Action Plan, endorsed by the G20 in September 2013. The mandate for the BEPS project was stated in the Tax Annex of the G20 St Petersburg Declaration:

> First, changes to international tax rules must be designed to address the gaps between different countries' tax systems, while still respecting the sovereignty of each country to design its own rules.
>
> Second, the existing international tax rules on tax treaties, permanent establishment, and transfer pricing will be examined to ensure that profits are taxed where economic activities occur and value is created.
>
> Third, more transparency will be established, including through a common template for companies to report to tax administrations on their worldwide allocation of profits and tax.
>
> Fourth, all the actions are expected to be delivered in the coming 18 to 24 months. Developing countries must reap the benefits of the G20 tax agenda.

These are ambitious and far-reaching aims, and the timetable for achieving them is extremely rapid compared with the usual slow pace of international tax rule changes. However, the Action Plan envisages only patching up the existing system.[11]

The BEPS Action Plan proposes 15 action points, of which nine are on substantive issues, and six are aspects of coordination or procedures. The latter action points include a *study on the digital economy*, which will in effect be a check on whether the other action points can deal effectively with this issue, perhaps supplemented by indirect taxes. Another is the *collection of better data* on the extent of international tax avoidance. Two more concern transparency: the development of *model provisions for disclosure of 'aggressive tax planning' strategies* and *improving transfer pricing documentation requirements*. The last of these is potentially very significant, as it now subsumes the G20 mandate to establish a global template for multinationals to prepare and submit a country-by-country report for all countries where they do business, as discussed above.

To help deal with conflicts between states, it is proposed to *strengthen the 'mutual agreement procedure'*, probably by introducing compulsory arbitration, although this has been resisted until now especially by developing countries. If there is little clarity or agreement on the rules to be applied, referring disputes to arbitrators to decide would be unhelpful, and perhaps dangerous. Further, the secrecy of these procedures undermines their legitimacy, and creates public distrust and suspicion of private deals by revenue authorities with big business.

Finally, and most ambitiously, a group of international lawyers are to develop a *multilateral instrument*, as a means of more rapid implementation of proposals which would otherwise require renegotiation of many bilateral treaties. While this is potentially far-reaching, the idea is legally problematic, and could result in a complex tangle of interactions between treaties and domestic law. It could also act as a brake on developing radical proposals, since such a treaty would have to be accepted and ratified by as many states as possible, so its content could tend to the least common denominator.

Of the nine substantive action points, the first group of four proposes to establish 'coherence of international tax standards' and concerns issues on which the CFA has done little or no previous work. A second group aims to restore the 'full effects and benefits of international standards' by modifying tax rules 'to more closely align the allocation of income with the economic activity that generates that income'. Three further action points concern the perennial problem of transfer pricing, and aim to continue and extend the revision of the Guidelines already under way since 2010, especially concerning the attribution of income to intangibles.

This Action Plan aims only to try to repair the current system, and cannot remedy its fundamental flaws, which result from the separate entity/arm's length principle in tax treaties. In paragraph 14 it explicitly rejects any move towards 'formulary apportionment'. The main objection is that, whatever its technical merits, it would be difficult or impossible to reach political agreement on such a system. Yet the attempt to strengthen the existing system in the Action Plan is also fraught with political difficulties. Indeed in many respects it is a recipe for generating conflicts between states, as each tries to modify or interpret the rules to grab a larger share of the tax base. The difference is that the reform plan defers the political conflicts and transfers them into the highly technical context of the CFA. No doubt there are many who will hope that over time the political spotlight will move on, perhaps even that the fiscal crises will dissipate, and the pressures for effective solutions will relax. It is very unlikely that political pressures will melt away, but the challenge for tax justice campaigners is to combine those pressures with proposals for more effective solutions.

An Alternative Approach: Unitary Taxation

Applying further patches to existing rules now seems futile. What is clearly necessary is to reorient international tax rules and place them on a more realistic foundation, which can treat multinationals as single firms, instead of being based on the unrealistic fiction that they are a loose collection of separate and independent entities in each country. A number of proposals with this perspective have already been put forward. The most comprehensive is unitary taxation with formula apportionment (UT). This is widely accepted as a superior approach in principle.[12] Although not without its difficulties, it is in many ways a more practical and effective alternative.[13]

Such an approach has a long history. It has been used for state taxes in federal systems with unified markets, such as Canada, Switzerland and the United States. It was developed in California to stop Hollywood film studios siphoning profits out by using distribution affiliates in Nevada. Today, all 47 US states which have a corporate income tax use formula apportionment, although following a campaign in the 1980s, non-US multinationals can choose to have it limited to their US business at 'water's edge'.

The European Union now has a fully worked-out proposal for a Common Consolidated Corporate Tax Base (CCCTB), developed by the European Commission over several years in consultation with business representatives and specialists. It was approved, with some amendments, by the European Parliament in April 2012, and since then has been under technical examination by the Council of Ministers. The proposal could certainly be improved, especially by extending its scope to deal more effectively with avoidance using non-EU tax havens.[14] This could be done by requiring a worldwide combined report, discussed further below. Nevertheless, if adopted it would go a long way towards dealing with many of the avoidance devices, such as the use of dual-resident affiliates in Ireland (the 'double-Irish') and conduit companies in the

Netherlands (the 'Dutch sandwich') discussed in Chapter 1. It is not surprising that Ireland and the Netherlands have opposed the proposal, but it is regrettable that others, including successive UK governments, have been sceptical or hostile, due to an unreasoning Europhobia.[15] A CCCTB would restore national powers of effective taxation of multi-nationals and hence enhance both the effectiveness and the legitimacy of national taxes.

What is needed is a move towards a unitary approach to taxation of multinationals on a global basis. A workable UT system should have three components: combined reporting, profit apportionment, and a resolution procedure. Each can be introduced to some extent immediately, and could be refined gradually by building on existing provisions.

Combined Reporting

First, any company with a business presence in more than one country should be required to submit a Combined and Country by Country Report (CaCbCR) to each tax authority. This should include (i) consolidated worldwide accounts for the firm as a whole, taking out all internal transfers; (ii) details of all the entities forming the corporate group and their relationships, as well as of transactions between them; and (iii) data on its physical assets, employees, sales (by destination), and actual taxes paid, in each country where it has a business presence.

An enormous step towards achieving this was taken in 2013 in the calls made by the G8 and G20 world leaders for greater corporate tax transparency, discussed above. If the OECD could draw up an effective template, it could transform international taxation. At present tax officials starting from separate affiliate tax returns find it hard to see the big picture, and this is especially difficult for those in poorer countries. This measure will now ensure that for the first time the tax authorities of each country where a firm has a taxable business presence will have access to information on its activities, on both a global and a national basis.

Much work remains to be done to design an effective common template, especially to modify financial accounting standards so that they are appropriate for tax purposes, and to establish an adequate basis for true consolidated accounts.[16] Tax authorities need to establish appropriate procedures for requiring submission of this global report, although an international framework already exists through the Multilateral Convention on Mutual Administrative Assistance in Tax Matters, mentioned above. This will greatly facilitate closer cooperation between tax authorities in ensuring a more coordinated approach towards multi-national taxation, including exchange of more detailed information and where appropriate joint audits.

Full transparency of course requires that these global reports should be publicly available. Campaigners will fight for this. It remains to be seen whether business lobbies can muster sufficiently cogent arguments to resist publication. The first and most important step is to ensure that the scope of information made available to tax authorities is adequate for their purposes.

Profit Apportionment

Second, states can use the CaCbCR to decide on an appropriate apportionment of the profit. This also can build on existing practice. There is already considerable experience in applying formulaic apportionment both of fixed and shared costs, and of profits. In particular the profit-split method, which has been one of the five accepted transfer pricing methods in the OECD *Guidelines* since 1995, apportions aggregated profits of related firms according to appropriate 'allocation keys'.

The profit-split method has in practice been increasingly used, especially with the growing importance of intangibles. This has become an intractable issue because the OECD approach has exacerbated the difficulties created by the SE-ALP rule, by fetishising the very concept of 'intangibles'. The oligopolistic profits of multinationals are to a great extent due to their control of superior know-how, but a firm's knowledge or know-how is very much a result of synergy, and it is very hard to value the different contributions of different parts of the firm to that whole. This is so even when such knowledge can take the form of intellectual property, since this concept creates a misleading notion of the nature of innovation or creativity as individualised, episodic and discrete, instead of collective, continuous and cumulative.

Recognition of the difficulties led to a reconsideration of Chapter 6 of the *OECD Guidelines on Intangibles*, begun in 2010, which has now been reinforced by its inclusion as an action point in the BEPS project. The draft revised chapter of the *OECD Guidelines on Intangibles* issued a couple of weeks after the Action Plan – the final version is due in 2014 – does propose some long-overdue changes. It would move away from attribution of profits on intangibles on the basis of ownership, or provision of finance. This has enabled Google and others to accumulate enormous profits in low-tax countries such as Bermuda, due to the foresight of their tax advisers at an early stage in transferring the rights in its search algorithm to an affiliate resident there, and benefit from the 'double-Irish'/'Dutch sandwich' avoidance schemes. Instead, profits would be attributed according to each entity's contribution to 'value creation' through its 'functions performed, assets used, and risks assumed'. The extent to which any of these functions, assets and risk factors affects value is stated to depend on the facts and circumstances, to be decided ad hoc in each case. The draft is full of equivocation on how this can be done, on the one hand stating that as far as possible the starting point should be 'comparables', while also conceding that 'the identification of reliable comparables in many cases involving intangibles may be difficult or impossible'.[17] In fact, attribution of profits based on the contribution to 'value creation' will inevitably lead to greater use of the profit-split method.

Under the *OECD Guidelines*, the profit-split method apportions the aggregate profits of related entities using suitable 'allocation keys'. This approach should be extended, because at present it envisages aggregation at the level of transacting entities, whereas multinationals use more complex cross-linkages among affiliates. The OECD has preferred to limit the scope of profit-split, so that it is used only to apportion the 'residual' profit, that which remains after methods based on comparables have been applied as far as possible. It is not surprising that this is regarded as unsatisfactory and arbitrary by many. Treating it as a fall-back means that tax officials and advisers must still struggle to try to find 'comparables', even though they know that genuine comparables do not exist. Yet when it comes to applying profit split to the residual, they are left to haggle like traders in the bazaar, since the method has not been systematised.

Several tax authorities prefer not to waste time on complex evaluation of comparables, and focus mainly on profit-split. Developing country tax administrations in particular say that suitable comparables are hard to find, and prefer to use profit apportionment methods, which can better take into account the real contribution of affiliates to the global value chain. India and China, for example, emphasise the role of 'location-specific advantages', and consider both profit-split and even in some circumstances a 'global formulary approach' as a 'realistic and appropriate option'.[18]

A broader application of the profit-split method could be developed through advance price agreements (APAs) with individual firms. Many countries offer APA programmes, and they can be negotiated with two or more states where appropriate. A formula-based apportionment method has been applied for some 20 years in the finance sector, using APAs with banks to allocate the profits of global trading conducted by offices in different time-zones over 24 hours.[19] If firms such as Apple, Amazon, Google and Starbucks would really like to pay a fair level of taxes wherever they do business, they too could enter into APAs and agree an appropriate apportionment.

The experience of using profit-split and APAs could be combined with proper research to determine the most appropriate apportionment formulae. The most balanced approach seems to be a three-factor formula, using physical assets, employees and sales.[20] The assets factor should be limited to physical assets, as in the CCCTB, excluding intangibles. As discussed above, these are elusive to define and value, and can easily be relocated. Some argue that there is no need to include assets, since they are of decreasing importance in the 'weightless economy'.

Nevertheless, a general formula designed to apply as far as possible to all sectors should include an assets factor, provided it is indeed limited to physical assets. As regards employees, US states use employee payroll costs not headcount, but this would be inappropriate internationally, because of the greater wage differences. The proposed CCCTB would use a 50:50 weighting of payroll and headcount, which seems appropriate. Sales should be quantified according to the location of the customer. Sellers can and do identify the location of their customers for delivery purposes, and for sales of services and digital products at least through their billing address. Although customers may use accounts based in tax havens for such purchases, they would have no reason to do so in order to reduce the tax liability of the sellers.

Some argue that states would aim to use a weighting which emphasises the factor that produces the most revenue for them, so they would never agree on a formula. In fact states need to consider the effects on investment. Hence in the United States the trend has been towards a greater emphasis on the sales factor, which does not act as a deterrent on inward investment. A balance between production and consumption factors seems best. This could be locked in by adopting a two-stage apportionment: an initial allocation to each country by production factors, then apportionment of the residual by sales. Special formulae may be needed for specific sectors, but it should be remembered that tax on business profits is only one instrument. For extractive industries in particular it must be supplemented by rent taxation, using royalties and/or a rent resource tax.

It should be stressed that this approach does not seek to *attribute* profit, since it assumes that the profits of an integrated firm result from its overall synergies, and economies of scale and scope. It *allocates* profits according to the measurable physical presence of the firm in each country.

Some argue that firms could still reorganise themselves to minimise their taxes, which of course is correct. However, if the factors in the allocation formula are based on real physical contacts with a country, such reorganisations would involve actual relocation. Thus, while competition to attract investment would not be ended, under unitary taxation this competition would become more sharply focused on attracting genuine production. Furthermore, if firms choose to divest some operations such as retail sales to truly independent third parties, they would lose the profits of synergy and scale. It is hard to imagine a company such as Apple being willing to transfer to a truly independent wholesaler in a low-tax country a significant slice of its profits. Jurisdiction to tax should be based on not the physical presence concept of permanent establishment (PE), but a broad business presence test, to include sales via a website.

States would remain free to choose their own marginal tax rates. Hence countries could compete to attract genuine investment rather than formation of paper entities aimed at subverting the taxes of other countries. Harmonisation of the tax base definition would greatly reduce the existing damaging forms of competition to attract investments by offering special exemptions. UT would therefore eliminate harmful tax competition, while allowing countries to make genuine choices between attracting investment in production and generating revenues from corporate taxation. Such a system would of course not be perfect, but aligning tax rules more closely to the economic reality of integrated firms operating in liberalised world markets would make it simpler and more effective.

Resolving Conflicts

The third important element is a procedure for the resolution of disagreements and conflicts between states. This is already provided for in the mutual agreement procedure (MAP) in tax treaties. But it needs to be improved and extended to include negotiation of APAs. This could increasingly be done on a multilateral basis, which is favoured by some multinationals. Developing countries should strengthen or develop their APA negotiation programmes. Investment in expertise for these would be much more cost-effective than developing expertise in transfer pricing adjustments based on comparables.

These procedures could also be considerably improved. This is one of the OECD's BEPS action points, with proposals to introduce a provision long sought by firms: compulsory and binding arbitration. This has been resisted until now, especially by developing countries, and for good reason. If there is little clarity or agreement on the rules to be applied, referring disputes to arbitrators to decide would be unhelpful and perhaps dangerous. The secrecy of these procedures undermines their legitimacy, and creates public distrust and suspicion of private deals by revenue authorities with big business. The MAP is at present very secretive, and decisions often involving hundreds of millions or even billions of dollars are not published. The case of GlaxoSmithKline, summarised in Box 10.1, did become public because it had to be litigated. It gives an idea of the enormous sums involved, and the arbitrary nature of the rules now used to decide their allocation.

The secrecy of both MAP processes and APAs greatly increases the power of frequent actors in these processes – that is, the international tax and accounting firms – to the great detriment of the system as a whole. Publication of both would be a great step towards a system which could both provide, and more importantly be seen to deliver, a fair international allocation of tax.

Box 10.1 *The GlaxoSmithKline case*

The pharmaceutical company GlaxoSmithKline was assessed for US$5.2 billion in back taxes and interest by the US Internal Revenue Service (IRS) in 2004 related to profits from its anti-ulcer drug Zantac. Glaxo claimed it should be paid a refund of US$1 billion, so there was a difference of over $6 billion. The drug itself had resulted from research done in the United Kingdom, but the IRS argued that a significant proportion of the high revenue it generated in the United States was attributable to Glaxo's US marketing intangibles.

It is indeed true that big pharma companies actually spend more on testing and marketing than they do on research into drugs. These elements, though, are interdependent: the pharmaceutical compound invented in the laboratory is greatly refined in the development and testing process, and benefits from the feedback received from its use in clinical practice, while large sales also depend on promotion and advertising. In reality it is very hard to decide what proportion of the total profit can be attributed to any of these activities; the big pharma firms benefit from the synergy of combining them all. The dispute was finally settled with a payment by Glaxo of US$3.4 billion.[21]

Conclusions

The reforms to the current system now being developed by the OECD, discussed in the second section of this chapter, could, if they are developed and applied in a determined way, make significant improvements to the system.[22] However, the OECD's Action Plan does not include some measures which could be particularly helpful for developing countries, such as withholding taxes and taxation of services.

For some of the measures included in the Action Plan the OECD is unlikely to propose solutions that would be strong enough or appropriate for developing countries, especially the definition and attribution of profits to a permanent establishment, and limitation of deductions. Strengthening of such aspects would be difficult for individual countries to undertake, because they may be considered a deterrent to inward investment, so collective action by groups of countries would be preferable. This should be facilitated and supported by bodies such as the UN Tax Committee, the International Monetary Fund's (IMF's) Tax Policy Division, and regional organisations, such as the African Tax Administration Forum (ATAF) and the Inter-American Centre of Tax Administrations (CIAT).

Increasing corporate tax revenues would be a significant boost to government coffers, as they account for 8–10 per cent of tax revenues in OECD countries and about twice that in developing countries. These revenues have remained more or less stable over the past 20–30 years despite both major reductions of tax rates and the big increases of corporate profits in proportion to GDP.[23] Hence there has been a significant decline in corporate taxes paid in relation to profits. Though it is difficult to estimate the actual losses incurred through tax avoidance by multinationals, the international expansion of such firms since the 1950s has itself been partly due to their ability to avoid taxes on retained earnings, as explained in Chapter 1. Avoidance has become more sophisticated with the shift to the digital economy and the knowledge society. This accounts for the continuing relative decline in revenues from corporate taxes.

These losses from corporate tax avoidance also result from the exploitation of the offshore tax-haven and secrecy system. Research conducted for the TJN has estimated the total amount of global financial wealth, excluding assets such as yachts and other property, held in the tax-free offshore system at $21–31 trillion in 2010. Around one-third of this is attributable to developing countries.[24] Bringing these enormous accumulations of capital back into the tax net would transform government revenues, in both developed and developing countries.

Beyond the direct revenue gains, ending the systematic tax avoidance by multinationals through the tax havens and offshore secrecy system would have many more benefits. The system sustains a vast army of professionals engaged in avoidance and evasion not only of tax but also of banking and financial and other forms of regulation, resulting in enormously wasteful expenditures for both firms and governments. Its removal would help to restore the legitimacy of taxation. This is seriously undermined when the largest and most important corporations are seen to be free-riding by failing to contribute to the state provision of collective services, including education, communications and transport, from which they benefit. It would also re-establish a more level playing field between the large multinationals and SMEs which are local and national, as well as removing distortions on investment decisions by the multinationals themselves.

These techniques of tax avoidance have also distorted the finance sector. They were a significant element in shadow banking and related practices which contributed to the excessive leverage which helped to feed the bubble that caused the financial crash of 2007–09. Since the techniques and facilities devised by the tax avoidance industry, using the offshore tax haven and secrecy system, are also used for all kinds of evasion, not only of taxes, but of other laws, including money laundering for crime, corruption and terrorism, measures now being taken to try to deal with all these activities would be easier to enforce if multinationals ceased to use the offshore system.

The taxation of multinational companies is a complex and difficult area, as this chapter has demonstrated, but there are some key objectives which need to be stressed and must form part of any campaign for reform:

- Transparency in the national and international taxation systems must be the initial objective through the implementation of the proposed country-by-country reporting rules.
- The longer-term goal must be the adoption of a unitary taxation system for all multinational companies, based on the apportionment of the full range of actual business operations in each jurisdiction.
- The underlying objective must be to achieve an increased and fairer contribution by multinational corporations to state revenues in both developed and developing countries.

11

Reforming Systems of Governance, Accounting and Auditing

It might be expected that the systems of corporate governance, accounting and auditing would be designed so as to facilitate competent business management to ensure their company survives in the short term and grows and prospers long term, for the benefit of the common good as well as the immediate stakeholders. This was the expectation of those who prepared and implemented the initial company law statutes in 1844 and 1856. That approach has been followed in successive company legislation, though with some continuing ambiguities, down to the most recent UK Companies Act of 2006. But if this has been the intention, the outcome has been far from satisfactory.

From the start of incorporation there were suspicions that the providers of equity capital were seeking to manipulate affairs for their own exclusive advantage. In the 1840s and 1850s there were significant frauds and losses by the investing public in the promotion and sale of shares in railway companies. A century ago the first 'robber barons' emerged in the United States, financially manipulating big business to their advantage. Their dominance led, inevitably it seemed with hindsight, to the 1929 Wall Street crash and subsequent Great Depression. Those lessons led to corporate legislation and governance systems aimed at rebuilding competitive markets and an efficient corporate sector backed by prudent finance which would contribute to the maintenance of full employment and the common good. All this is explained by Keynesian economics.

Over the last four decades, those carefully constructed limits have been progressively demolished. The holders of equity capital have regained precedence, and exploited that position to the detriment of the common good and the interests of all other stakeholders. To ensure executive decisions are taken in their interest, they have converted executives into shareholders by the implementation of share option bonus schemes to achieve a coincidence of interest in maximising shareholder value.

The resulting growth and dominance of financial interests, promoted and manipulated by a growing body of financial intermediaries, has had a serious impact on real economic enterprise and development. The reversal of monetary flows from companies to shareholders, rather than from dispersed shareholders to companies to make large-scale investment, has produced a 'multi-trillion dollar transfer of cash from United States corporations to their shareholders over the past 10 years'.[1] In the United Kingdom there has been a similar proportional flow of funds. In both countries the number of public companies has almost halved over the same ten-year period. In the United States the numbers decreased by 38 per cent, with IPOs down by over two-thirds and SME IPOs down 80 per cent.[2]

The financial crisis in 2007–09 and its aftermath have revealed serious weaknesses in corporate governance which appear to have contributed to the crash. The OECD Steering Group on Corporate Governance has argued that weak governance was a major cause.[3] The UK Treasury Select Committee has supported that view, highlighting in particular governance failures in banking.[4] The Financial Services Authority's Turner Review[5] and HM Treasury's Walker Review[6] both highlighted failings in governance of companies and financial institutions, and flagged up the urgent need for improvements in governance effectiveness. It seems that systems of corporate governance, and associated accounting and auditing processes, have been complicit with both exploitative capital and its subsequent collapse. This situation requires explanation and reform.

Corporate Governance and the Law

The original purpose of establishing a public company was to enable sufficient finance to be raised to fund major new projects such as railways and large-scale manufacture. Funding such projects depended on raising finance from many dispersed contributors. The risk was recognised that major shareholders might take advantage of the rest and thereby defeat the object of the dispersed shareholding system. Initially those suspicions were eased by the adoption of democratic voting – one member, one vote – irrespective of the number of shares held and with no proxy voting permitted. In the United States, democratic voting was said to be justified by the 'American fear of unbridled power, as possessed by large landholders and dynastic wealth, as well as by government'.[7]

An Act of Parliament in 1776 explained that the purpose of such practical limits on the power of large shareholders was to protect 'the permanent welfare of companies' from being 'sacrificed to the partial and interested views of the few.'[8] Similarly in Germany a commentator in 1837 suggested the democratic approach to voting had a profound impact on the way the corporation was managed compared with the plutocratic one share, one vote system which favoured those with large holdings.[9] Votes at general meetings were commonly taken on the democratic basis of a show of hands. However, these protections against the unbridled power of the few were gradually removed. By the late 19th century one share, one vote had become almost universal.

The duties of company directors have also been developed and interpreted in ways that favour short-term finance rather than long-term economic interests. Until recently these duties were described largely through individual legal decisions, and were generally expressed as being to act 'bona fide in the best interests of the company', though the precise meanings of 'bona fide' and 'best interests' were never finally agreed in the courts. But there is no law suggesting that directors owe a legal duty to act as agents of the shareholders. A review of the legal position in Anglo-American jurisdictions found just one item of US case law in 1919 that supported the agency doctrine, and that was so weak it had only ever been cited once in court. Nor did the review find any statute law supporting the agency relationship of directors with shareholders.[10]

In the United Kingdom the general duties owed by a director of any company were reformulated in the Companies Act 2006 and clearly stated to be to the company, not to the shareholders,[11] though the Act retains some ambiguity:

A director of a company must act in the way *he* [emphasis supplied] considers, in good faith, would be most likely to promote the success of the company for the benefit of its members as a whole, and in doing so have regard (amongst other matters) to —

(a) the likely consequences of any decision in the long term,
(b) the interests of the company's employees,
(c) the need to foster the company's business relationships with suppliers, customers and others,
(d) the impact of the company's operations on the community and the environment,
(e) the desirability of the company maintaining a reputation for high standards of business conduct; and
(f) the need to act fairly as between members of the company.[12]

US law follows a similar line: the duties and responsibilities of company directors are defined by state legislations which typically include the duty to act in good faith in the best interests of the corporation and its shareholders, having regard to various other interests.

The precise meanings of 'success of the company' and 'good faith' have yet to be defined in court, and there has not been relevant case-law to demonstrate how the 2006 definition of duties might be interpreted by the courts. Even so, it does seem clear that if there is any conflict between the company's interests and those of the shareholders, then the company's interests should prevail.

The impact of the 2006 Act is severely limited by the fact that the only people who can seek to enforce a breach of duty by a director, if the board itself acting for the company has failed to do so, are the shareholders. In most mergers and acquisitions, as in the cases of the takeover of Cadbury by Kraft, and Boots the Chemist by the private equity multinational Kohlberg Kravis Roberts, the shareholders are the prime, if not sole, beneficiaries. They are unlikely to take action against the company directors for not acting in the shareholders' best interests. Consequently, the mainstream shareholder primacy perspective in management circles and business schools continues in complete disregard for the 2006 Act.

There is a further deficiency in the current legal regime which would have been avoided had democratic voting been maintained among members. There is a discontinuity in voting power as individual or concerted shareholdings rise above the 50 per cent threshold. This changes the nature of ownership, and the effective legal status of the company itself. A shareholder's liability is discharged in full when the shares are paid for. There is no ongoing liability to the company. The shares grant entitlement to dividends and to the potential for capital growth, which may or may not materialise, but in normal circumstances the shareholders have ownership rights only over their shares. They do not own the company, which is a legal entity in its own right. It has some of the same legal rights and responsibilities as a person, such as the right to sue and be sued in its own right, to enter into contracts and to maintain its operations by skilful management and investment. However, when individual or concerted share ownership exceeds 50 per cent of the total equity, the nature of that relationship changes. The holder or holders of a majority of the shares have effective control, and the company becomes more like an item of private property in that the controlling shareholder(s) can treat the company's assets more as if they were in their private ownership.

The practical impacts of that discontinuity are clearly apparent in mergers and acquisitions, but the legal implications do not yet appear to have been fully explored. There are provisions which purport to protect minority shareholders from prejudicial or unfair treatment by a majority,[13] but in decisions over the future development or sale of the company or its assets, majority rule is the accepted norm. As will be seen, this often excludes any real consideration of the longer-term interests of the company, its employees or customers, or the community in which it operates.

Governance and Codes of Practice

It might be thought that some of these deficiencies would be mitigated by the growing number of codes of practice on corporate governance and social responsibility. The motivation behind the development of the first code of best practice, appended to the *Cadbury Report on the Financial Aspects of Corporate Governance* in 1992, was directly related to the apparently increasing abuse and fraud perpetrated by some company directors and executives during the 1980s.[14] The *Cadbury Report* made specific reference in its preface to three infamous cases: Guinness, Maxwell and BCCI.

The Guinness share-trading fraud involved its chief executive, Ernest Saunders, and other senior executive and non-executive directors trying to fix prices on the London Stock Exchange by using the good offices of a US insider trader, Ivan Boesky, in order to reduce the cost of acquiring the Distillers Company. Robert Maxwell, already disgraced and identified by the Department of Trade and Industry inspectors as a person unfit to be a director of a British company, had managed to revive his corporate career, but in the aftermath of his assumed suicide he was found to have stolen millions of pounds from his companies and their pension funds. BCCI collapsed amid revelations of extensive fraud and criminal activities involving drug dealing and money laundering. These were just three notorious examples of a growing list of corporate criminality which was hitting the headlines in both Britain and the United States, and which led to the Cadbury initiative on corporate governance.

The expressed aims of the Cadbury Code were to inhibit corporate criminality, restrain directors' pay, and align directors' interests with those of their shareholders by emphasising the principles of openness, integrity and accountability. It is not clear which was the more powerful motivation in drafting this and other codes. While criminality and excessive directors' pay continued to expand with little restraint, the codes have been more successful in persuading directors that it was their duty to focus on satisfying short-term shareholder interests.

The *Cadbury Report* was narrowly focused on the financial aspects of corporate governance rather than any wider concerns. It was rapidly followed by similar codes of practice in most advanced economies, so that there is now hardly a developed or developing nation without some explicit code of governance practice.[15]

On accountability the *Cadbury Report* declared:

> The formal relationship between the shareholders and the board of directors is that the shareholders elect the directors, the directors report on their stewardship to the shareholders and the shareholders appoint the auditors to provide an external check on the directors' financial statements. Thus the shareholders as owners of the company elect the directors to run the business on their behalf and hold them accountable for its progress. The issue for corporate governance is how to strengthen the accountability of boards of directors to shareholders.[16]

Thus, acceptance of the agency relationship was foundational to the Cadbury code, even though there was no explicit statement that 'to run the business on their behalf' meant maximising shareholder value. The neoclassical perspective was simply assumed in preference to the well-established law requiring directors to 'promote the success of the company'. That bias is also revealed in the assertion that shareholders elect the directors. The reality is that when a public company is first granted a stock exchange listing, the directors are already in place prior to its shares being offered for sale. Subsequent appointments are then usually agreed by the board and subsequently offered for confirmation at the AGM. Similarly, the statement that shareholders are the owners of the company is contradicted in standard legal texts, which emphasise that the ownership is of share certificates enjoying limited liability. The question clearly arises whether the code was designed as a genuine attempt to fulfil its three stated aims, or was a carefully mounted defence of shareholder primacy.

The substance of the code was concerned with more detailed arrangements for the board of directors, including the separation of the roles of chairman and chief executive; the independence of non-executive directors; limitations on the contracts of executive directors, disclosure of their pay, and the establishment of a remuneration committee made up wholly or mainly of non-executive directors; arrangements for public reporting and audit; and the establishment of an internal audit committee, as well as relationships with shareholders. This merely reflected what was already accepted as good practice.

A more significant issue was the approach to implementation. Publicly quoted companies on the London Stock Exchange were required either to comply or to explain and justify their non-compliance. Many in the financial establishment raised objections to the code, and many quoted companies opted for explanation rather than compliance, but there was limited guidance on what constituted a satisfactory explanation, and no indication of action to be taken if the explanation was unsatisfactory. Consequently the code appeared to have little practical effect.

Since 1992 successive British enquiries and reports have resulted in revisions to the existing codes of practice, culminating for the time being with the publication in 2012 of the Financial Reporting Council's *UK Corporate Governance Code*. This was developed in the light of experience during and after the 2007–09 financial crisis of notoriously high levels of remuneration for top managers and traders, as well as massively expensive taxpayer-funded bail-outs for the banking sector and 'quantitative easing' intended to revive the broader economy. Despite that severe learning experience, the new code focused its main attention on tying the company ever tighter to its shareholders, advocating that a senior independent director should meet with major shareholders in order to gain 'a balanced understanding of the issues and concerns of major shareholders'. This does not appear to have had much impact.

In reality successive codes have failed spectacularly to reduce corporate abuse and criminality or to rein in excessive remuneration for senior executives. That failure was acknowledged in the preface to the 2012 version, which stated that 'much more attention needs to be paid to following the spirit of the Code as well as its letter' and 'that the impact of shareholders in monitoring the Code could and should be enhanced by better interaction between the boards of listed companies and their shareholders'.

In reality there have always been limited opportunities for shareholders to have an active relationship with the companies they have invested in. Yet just as shareholding was changing and an active relationship was becoming less relevant to investors, the stewardship role of those controlling the shareholdings attracted increasing attention. The weak statements in the *Corporate Governance Code* are mirrored in the first *UK Stewardship Code*, which provides guidance on good practice for financial intermediaries managing assets on behalf of shareholders.[17] The aim was clearly to address the 'agency problem' – that some company directors were not focusing exclusively on maximising shareholder value – and the role institutional shareholders might play in solving the problem. However, the code ignores the fact that the investment professionals who control the management of most institutional shareholdings are more interested in short-term price movements than the long-term interests of the company, or of those shareholders who might be interested in improving the quality of its management, or protecting the longer-term interests of the members of pension funds and others who rely on regular stock market dividends.

Much of the overall lack of impact of these codes in practice results from the radical changes in the nature of shareholding since the 'big bang' deregulation of stock markets in 1986 and the computerisation of stock exchanges. Though the codes were produced after the 'big bang', the change in the nature of shareholding has been progressive, and much of it came after the publication of the *Cadbury Report*. As was explained in greater detail in Chapter 7, the management of shareholdings has become increasingly concentrated in the hands of fund managers and professional traders, who themselves exercise control largely without ownership, and often rely on computer programmes and algorithms. The factors which influence such trades have little to do with the underlying value of the security being traded, and everything to do with some guesstimate of its future value, often measured in fractions of a second.

One of the factors affecting this guesstimate is the current price movement of the security in question. As a result contagion is inherent, bubbles essential and bursts inevitable. It is estimated that 60–70 per cent of all trades are now completed by such ultra-fast systems.[18] This change has converted shareholding into a short-term speculative activity aimed at improving the trader's position on the relevant league table. Stewardship codes ignore this aspect of 'control without ownership', just as they ignore the dominance of ultra-fast automated and algorithmic trading systems.

So the impact of these British codes of practice appears to have been minimal. That seems to be acknowledged in the United States, where the emphasis has been more on legal restraints, with genuinely punitive sentencing and some willingness to apply the law. Numerous codes of practice have been developed at state level, though they too seem to be recognised as window-dressing. The emphasis in the main financial centres has been more on the development of law as an answer to criminality. Junk bond and insider trader Michael Milken, and loan and savings fraudster Charles Keating, topped the list of 1980s corporate criminals, while top executives at Enron, Worldcom and others, have joined the list of incarcerated fraudsters. The response of the Federal administration was to enact the Sarbanes–Oxley Act in 2002, which promised up to 20 years imprisonment for certain misdemeanours. The apparent willingness to use the law and imprison the guilty has had some effect. JP Morgan Chase has paid fines of over $25 billion in lieu of criminal charges.

The US approach appears in stark contrast with the voluntarist 'comply or explain' requirement of UK codes of practice. UK company legislation is replete with ambiguity. This should be eliminated and the consequences for transgression clarified as in the Sarbanes–Oxley Act. And though the practical reality may be less differentiated than might be expected, there is clearly a need for a major shift in regulatory strategy to impose very substantial penalties on those who break the rules. Criminal prosecutions may not always be practical, but the financial regulators and the non-statutory City authorities need to use their powers to exclude those guilty of abuse from any further involvement in publicly traded companies or the financial markets.

Auditing and Accounting

Accountants in their role as auditors are supposed to play a key role in the processes of corporate governance. Their primary task, as enshrined in legislation, is to check and report to shareholders on the annual financial statements produced by all major companies, and to certify that they present a true and fair view of the affairs of the company. If after due investigation auditors have any material reservations about that, they are required to qualify the accounts and draw the attention of shareholders to the deficiencies. Audit reports are not directly addressed to regulators, creditors, employees, pension scheme members and other stakeholders, but are used by them as they contain signals about corporate practices.

The practice of auditing deviates considerably from this. As was outlined in Chapter 2, auditors rarely do more than sign off on internally produced corporate accounts, and have regularly failed to alert shareholders or investors of frauds, material financial mis-statements and the impending financial collapse of major public companies. The audit effort is invisible to outsiders, and auditor files are not available for public scrutiny. In this weak environment, profit-conscious auditors work closely with company directors and their audit committees. They are rarely in a strong position to challenge company directors because their fees depend on appeasement of directors. Auditing for the largest public companies throughout the world is dominated by the 'big four' accountancy firms – Deloitte & Touche, PricewaterhouseCoopers, KPMG and Ernst & Young – which also act as their business advisers. This has led to an increasingly cosy relationship between major companies and their auditors, in which the companies pay huge fees to their auditors for consultancy on financial engineering and tax avoidance. In return, the fee-dependent auditors are expected to facilitate the presentation of corporate accounts that give a rosy picture of corporate finances.

There are three major aspects of these relationships which require comprehensive reform. First, although the corporate laws provide a broad framework for the preparation and filing of company accounts, the details are left to private-sector organisations dominated by large corporations and accountancy firms. Second, despite periodic scandals, the regulatory system to ensure that auditors are truly independent of the companies that they audit is weak. And third, there is currently no direct channel of communication between auditors and shareholders, and no means by which shareholders and other stakeholders can either hold the auditors to account or require them to provide more detailed information on matters of concern.

The first required reform is that accounting rules and standards should be made by a body that is representative of a plurality of social interests. It should not be dominated by accounting or corporate interests, but should ensure that the standards are the outcomes of negotiations and consensus rather than self-interest. This is currently not the case. The London-based International Accounting Standards Board (IASB) formulates International Financial Reporting Standards (IFRSs). It is a private limited liability company owned by the IFRS Foundation, registered in the US tax haven of Delaware. The main motive for this structure is to avoid UK taxes on the revenues of the IASB.[19] National bodies, such as the UK-based Financial Reporting Council (FRC), simply follow the IFRSs.

The IASB is primarily funded by the 'big four' accounting firms and large corporations, although it also receives some public monies from the European Union. Private-sector bodies are always vulnerable to pressure from their funders. Following the 2001 demise of US energy giant Enron, for example, it came to light that the IASB had asked Enron for a $500,000 donation. Enron had indicated its willingness to provide money in return for increasing its influence on the IASB.[20]

The result is that the IASB board and personnel for working parties and committees come primarily from big business, and there is little representation from other stakeholders. This has enabled big business to control the agenda, and is one of the reasons for the production of disastrous accounting standards which enabled banks to recognise unrealised profits, overstate assets and move large tranches of assets and liabilities off balance sheets.

This is obviously unacceptable. Accounting practices are deeply implicated in the distribution of wealth, income and risks, and only democratically accountable bodies should have a mandate to shape the landscape. The IASB does not fit that requirement, and should be replaced by a body under democratic control. All accounting standards must be specifically approved by national governing bodies. If international accounting standards are to be developed, then that task should be delegated to a committee of the United Nations, subject to ratification by national parliaments. No accounting standard should be issued without consideration of the potential harmful effects. The standard-setting body could be funded by increasing the cost of filing annual accounts and returns for large companies and through general taxation revenues. All standard-setting boards, working parties and committees should meet in the open, and their minutes and reports should be publicly available.

The same should apply to auditing standards. These are now largely formulated by the International Auditing and Assurance Standards Board (IAASB), an offshoot of the International Federation of Accountants (IFAC). The IFAC is dominated by professional accountancy bodies and major accounting firms, and thus has no independence from the auditing industry. National standard setters, such as the UK Financial Reporting Council, are subordinated to the standards issued by the IAASB. So auditing standards are often the lowest common denominator, as auditing firms seek to legitimise their in-house practices rather than deal with challenges from a dynamic business environment.

The current auditing standards cover over 3,000 pages, but there is not a single line on auditor accountability to any stakeholder. Auditing standards should be formulated by a body representative of a plurality of social interests. Accountants should not have an inbuilt majority on this body. The standards should be the outcome of negotiations and consensus amongst stakeholders, and the procedural and approval structures for accounting standards should also apply to the work of all auditing standards bodies.

Ensuring the effective independence of auditors is equally important. Auditors for large companies should not be permitted to sell any consultancy services to their audit clients.[21] Despite numerous scandals, the most recent proposals for reform within the European Union have been unduly influenced by the auditing industry and remain inadequate.[22] The main provisions would be a prohibition on the sale of some selected non-auditing services by auditors to their audit clients, stringent limits on tax advice and on services linked to the financial and investment strategy of the audit client, and a cap of 70 per cent on the fees generated for non-audit services other than those prohibited, based on a three-year average. This is an invitation for creative games, and auditors will still continue to audit the very transactions that they themselves have created. Tax avoidance schemes have already begun to be marketed as 'financial restructuring schemes', and will thus not easily be caught by the proposed reforms.

Real independence requires that auditors should act exclusively as auditors, and that means no consultancy work for audit clients. In other sectors, audits are carried out by immigration officers, health and safety inspectors, tax inspectors and fire safety officers, and none are allowed to sell consultancy, become agents of those they audit, or acquire a financial interest in the transactions subject to an audit. That discipline also needs to apply to company auditors. To prevent the development of cosy relationships, all large companies should be required to change their auditors every five years.[23]

Even more stringent rules should be applied in the financial sector, as it is so intertwined with the rest of the economy. Private accounting firms have been auditing banks for over 100 years, and the banking crash of 2007–09 showed that audit failures are now institutionalised. In this sector auditors need to be the eyes and ears of the regulators on a real-time basis. They should be present at all material locations on a daily basis, and scrutinise significant transactions. In a world of instantaneous movement of finance, ex-post audits are of little use, and accountancy firms have routinely failed to protect the interests of regulators, savers and borrowers. Financial sector audits should be conducted by a statutory regulator specifically created for that purpose, with unhindered real-time access to all files and working papers of the auditor. Parliamentary committees, such as the UK House of Common Treasury Committee, should regularly scrutinise the effectiveness of financial regulation, and as part of that should also examine the effectiveness of auditing arrangements.

This approach would help to expand the supply side of audits. It would reduce the size of big accounting firms and encourage meaningful competition in the auditing industry. Auditing firms would no longer be too large to inhibit regulators from taking effective action, which should include the possibility of closing down firms routinely involved in audit failures.

Action is also required to increase the accountability of all auditors. The cosy relationship with directors and audit committees needs to be replaced by one in which auditors are required to engage directly with shareholders and other stakeholders. Any of these should be entitled to call for a special audit on matters of current concern, such as the level of risk in a company's financial arrangements, its taxation arrangements or the potential impact of takeovers or mergers. A statutory system of this kind has long operated in France and is regularly used.[24]

Finally, auditors should be formally and effectively liable for the quality of their work. Producers of potato crisps and toffees have to ensure that their products are fit for consumption, and the same duty of care should apply to auditors. They should owe a duty of care to all stakeholders who reasonably place reliance on audit reports. The public bears the cost of audit failures, and should therefore be entitled to make an assessment of audit quality and auditor knowledge base. All audit files should be publicly available, together with the composition of audit teams, time spend on the job, communications with directors and explanations from and to directors on contentious issues. Auditing firms enjoy a state-guaranteed market for external auditing, and should be required to publish meaningful information about their affairs. This should include details of regulatory sanctions, fines, income from auditing and consultancy, and transfers of personnel to and from client companies.

In view of the power and influence of corporations on the daily lives of the people, we also need to move beyond traditional accounting and auditing. As the distinction between the state and corporations is blurred, major corporations should be subjected to the freedom of information laws and required to provide personal information held by them, as well information about the harmful effects of their products and services.

Alternative Ways Forward

Twenty years ago the upsurge of interest in corporate governance in the United Kingdom and the United States resulted from three main concerns: the damage being visited on the real economy by an excess of merger and acquisition deal-making, the excessive pay levels of directors when related to performance, and a perception that UK and US companies, notably in the manufacturing, high-technology and construction industries, were becoming increasingly uncompetitive compared with their main rivals in Japan and Germany, not to mention the emerging BRICS economies.[25]

The increased attention to governance over those past 20 years appears not to have reduced any of these concerns. The concentration on shareholder value has continued to increase in both the United Kingdom and the United States. Other jurisdictions, however, have been less focused on pursuing the neoliberal agenda. Japan and Germany have both, by quite different means, protected their real economy companies from predation by their financial sectors, and so have been less prone to unproductive and disruptive merger and acquisition activity, with the consequence that their manufacturing, high-tech and construction industries have remained more competitive than in the United Kingdom and the United States.

Japan's industrial development was linked to the network of industrial conglomerates known as *zaibatsu*, which controlled a large proportion of all Japanese capital assets, especially in heavy industries such as iron and steel, shipbuilding and construction. These were family-owned holding companies, at the top of a pyramid of subsidiary companies, controlling majority shares in subsidiaries which owned majority shares in their subsidiaries. However, each operating company retained some independence and was protected from external takeovers. There were also horizontal cross-shareholdings which increased the impenetrability of the system. There was invariably a lead bank included in the shareholdings of the *zaibatsu* founding families, which provided, or underwrote, the financial needs of member firms.

After the Second World War, the US occupation administration disbanded the *zaibatsu*, and tried to establish US-style dispersed share ownership, but this initiative lasted less than a decade. By the mid-1950s, the old *zaibatsu* form of organisation had re-emerged in the shape of less formal networks referred to as *keiretsu*, which provided natural partners for firms in their financing arrangements and in their supply chains and distribution systems, and offered protection against the threat of hostile foreign takeovers.

Free market ideology suggests the Japanese model is anti-competitive and should therefore not work – but it appears to work well. Manufacturers in the Japanese model benefit from real competition, but are at the same time protected from the predatory merger and acquisition deal-making which is so much a feature of Anglo-American business. Although it is part of Japanese corporate culture, the *keiretsu* type of organisation, which offers protection from predatory financial intermediaries, could be adopted anywhere. Germany's industrial culture also provides protection from the short-term, deal-oriented and shareholder value maximising culture of the United Kingdom and the United States. Germany's orientation, both before and after reunification, has been social democratic, and that, at least in part, explains the difference in its corporate governance.

While the free market culture has led to an expanding and dominant financial sector in Britain, the culture in Germany resulted in an outwardly less successful but more secure financial sector and a more successful and secure real economy. Germany is the world's fourth largest manufacturer. In comparison the United Kingdom is now achieving less than half Germany's manufacturing output, and much of the UK manufacturing sector is no longer British-owned.

These differences penetrate very deeply into the nuts and bolts of corporate practice. One significant difference is that engineers rather than accountants tend to lead the management teams in German manufacturing companies.[26] As a result they are more interested in investing in effective production rather than short-term profitability.

This different culture has also had an effect on accounting practice. The primary focus of British accounting is to provide an apparently transparent picture of the company's affairs for the benefit of shareholders. In Germany, on the other hand, the focus has always been on the protection of creditors. Accounting norms for the valuation of assets highlight this difference. British balance sheets include properties at their latest professional valuation, whereas German law has required property to be included in the balance sheet at the lower of cost or market price. This allows German companies to accumulate large hidden reserves, which can be utilised as and when company management deem them to be really needed, rather than managers being under pressure to pay them over to shareholders at the first opportunity. The German approach has enabled its companies to take a longer-term perspective than is feasible under the neoclassical commitment to shareholder value and primacy.

A further critical difference which serves to protect the corporate sector from external financial opportunism is the two-tier board system, under which employees are represented on a supervisory board. Employee representation for large companies has been required by German law since 1870, under the statute which established the modern German form of stock corporation, the AG (AktienGesellschaft) publicly quoted company. The smaller, limited liability company, the GmbH (GesellschaftmitbeschränkterHaftung), is not required to have a supervisory board unless its employees regularly number more than 500. The two-tier system establishes a management board with responsibility for day-to-day running of the enterprise, and a supervisory board with various legally defined responsibilities including the appointment of management board members. From the outset the supervisory board was strictly separated from the management board, with no common membership allowed.

The supervisory board was established to protect the interests of various stakeholders including shareholders, employees and creditors, which were usually banks, as well as some stewardship of the public interest. Its members were chosen by those various constituents. Originally, employee representatives on the supervisory boards of major companies held a third of the board membership. But in 1976 this was increased to 50 per cent for companies with more than 2,000 employees, a change that suggests experience of employee membership was seen as positive. The legislation for AG companies now provides for supervisory boards of 20 members, ten of whom are elected by the shareholders, the other ten being employee representatives. The supervisory board not only appoints the members of the management board and approves their remuneration and sometime dismissal, but must also approve major strategic decisions, notably those involving mergers and acquisitions. Although this equality in representation remains controversial between management and trade union bodies, its contribution to the German economy has been highlighted and its retention recommended in a recent official report.[27]

The United States and the United Kingdom are focused on satisfying outside shareholder interests, while both Germany and Japan appear to be insider-oriented. The outsider-orientation has been associated with a decline in the level of inherent trust within the business sector, and a general acknowledgement by sociologists of a decline in social cohesion. Specifically, there has been a decline in society's confidence in institutions, such as corporations and institutional investment organisations.[28]

A system of employee representation on the unitary boards of companies employing 2,000 or more in Britain was recommended by the Bullock Committee on Industrial Democracy in 1977. The Bullock proposal was for the number of employee representatives to equal the number of shareholder representatives on the board, and for them to be selected solely through trade union machinery, with only unionised employees influencing the choice of employee directors.[29] Despite the German example, the proposal was strenuously opposed by management interests and in the end also rejected by trade unions. This was clearly a missed opportunity to rebalance corporate governance in the United Kingdom.

The notion of governance combining both internal and external aspects has been part of the prolonged discussions which culminated in developing the legal form of the European company which became available throughout the European Union from 2004. The European company is an enabling format, allowing either a single management board of directors, or a two-tier system comprising both an executive board and a supervisory board, including employee representatives, as in Germany. The extent of employee representation on the supervisory board has varied in different EU member states, as have the voting rights attached to different classes of company shares.

Adoption of the European company two-tier board structures in major companies would provide a better model for protecting not only the interests of the stakeholders represented, but also the public at large, from predation by sectional financial interests. The European company would provide a more balanced representation of interests than is currently enjoyed, or was recommended by the Bullock Committee. The aims of the European company legislation to create a European company with its own legislative framework were expressed as follows:

> This will allow companies incorporated in different Member States to merge or form a holding company or joint subsidiary, while avoiding the legal and practical constraints arising from the existence of fifteen different legal systems. This legislative framework also provides for the involvement of employees in European companies, giving due recognition to their place and role in the business.[30]

Within the European Union, and its now 27 different jurisdictions, the orientation is specifically towards the formal recognition of company employees as well as shareholders. It is an enabling format, allowing a two-tier system comprising both an executive board and a supervisory board. The executive board is intended to focus on operational issues and is chaired by a CEO, while the supervisory board is responsible for appointing and removing members of the executive board, for their remuneration and for their general supervision. The supervisory board is all non-executive and chaired by the company chairperson.

While there was previously no single European standard of governance practice, the concept of two-tier boards of directors had long been common, with executive directors on the management board, and non-executives, including employee representatives, serving on the separate supervisory board. The extent of employee representation on the supervisory board has varied in different EU member states, as have the voting rights attached to different classes of company shares. Nevertheless it is clear that practice across Europe shares a broad orientation of governance responsibilities, in contrast to the simple shareholder-centred approach. Adoption of the two-tier European company system would both provide protection from financial predation for real-economy companies, and would introduce some balance of the interests of different stakeholders, notably employees and shareholders.

Conclusion

The corporate population is not a homogeneous whole. It comprises a wide variety of firms with very different aims and values. There are professionally managed companies which seek to be efficient and competitive and to serve all their stakeholders fairly. There are also companies which are dedicated single-mindedly to the neoliberal aim of maximising shareholder wealth. There are firms focused on satisfying long-term goals and others focused totally on immediate gains. There are firms that are run with total integrity, and there are firms that are abusive, criminal and fraudulent.

Sumantra Ghoshal has argued that neoliberal ideology has provided the theoretical platform which is increasingly leading firms to pursue subservience to the shareholder. This has turned management itself into a monstrous caricature, which he describes as 'the ruthlessly hard-driving, strictly top-down, command-and-control focused, shareholder-value obsessed, win-at-any-cost business leader'.[31] He added that 'by propagating ideologically inspired amoral theories, business schools have actively freed their students from any sense of moral responsibility'.[32]

The first thing business schools need to do is to stop teaching the neoliberal ideology, but so far it has not happened. A report in July 2013 on business education confirmed that the theory is still being taught by business school staff. As Craig Smith, Insead Professor of Ethics and Social Responsibility, has put it, 'Students come in with a more rounded view of what managers are supposed to do, but when they go out, they think it's all about maximising shareholder value.'[33]

These are the future leaders of the industrial–financial–political nexus. If new managers continue to be taught in this way, they are likely to maintain the dominance of shareholder value ideology and the systems of governance, accounting and auditing described above, which facilitate predation and exploitation by the sectional interest of finance, rather than conducting business on the basis of having regard for the interests of all stakeholders including the community and the environment. This is, after all, what is required by law, albeit it was ambiguously expressed in the 2006 Companies Act.

The solutions within the established corporate sector, without prejudice to alternative mutual and not-for-profit structures, must include:

- eliminating ambiguity from company legislation, especially in respect of the duties of directors to work for the long-term interests of their companies rather than the exclusive interests of their shareholders
- the specification of serious consequences for transgression of legal or regulatory rules, and the strengthening of state regulators prepared to use the law to enforce standards of governance
- an end to business school teaching of the discredited neoliberal curriculum
- the inclusion in the business school curriculum of an accurate account of the current legal aspects of governance and the duties of company directors
- the introduction and promotion by tax incentives of a two-tier board structure for major companies, including supervisory boards with representatives of all stakeholders; this could be based on the existing European company or provided by specific UK (and other national) legislation
- separation of accounting from audit and from management consultancy to eliminate the conflicts of interest, a requirement on auditors to alert stakeholders to perceived risks on different underlying assumptions, the provision of direct communication between auditors and all stakeholders, and the development of procedures for special audits on matters of particular concern, as in France
- more effective provision for the break-up of monopolistic positions in sectors where competition has been compromised.

Banking Reform and the Control of Market Manipulation and Short-Termism

The main focus of this book is on the legal and practical structures and management of large corporate enterprises, but as was shown in Chapter 7, the structure and management of banks, the shadow banking system and stock markets have played a major role in generating and facilitating many of the most serious abuses. A comprehensive reform of the corporate sector must include measures to eliminate or at least minimise the adverse impact of the unacceptable practices that have developed in banking and market trading over the past few decades, notably since the 'big bang' deregulation of the stock market in 1986. This chapter is focused on the structural reforms and regulatory measures that are essential to the recreation of a financial sector, in both banking and market trading, that plays a positive rather than destructive role in the wider industrial and social economy.

The Impact of Financial Market Activities

The growth of financial markets over the last 20 years has had a profound impact on the UK economy. The massive international financial institutions that dominate the City of London have taken advantage of the deregulation and 'light touch' system of supervision to engage in highly risky leveraging of their assets. While in the short term this brought the dealers, managers and shareholders of these firms high returns, it was also a major generator of the financial crisis that had such an impact on the United Kingdom and the global economy more generally.

These large institutions also exercised considerable power and influence over their clients. Their ability to accrue information across their vast range of activities placed their clients in a situation of information asymmetry. The financial institutions sold products which they knew were risky to clients who were not informed of the degree of risk. Where they could, they manipulated prices, as in the LIBOR scandal. They pushed their dealers to the brink of legality, and sometimes beyond it, as they sought to push up earnings and maximise shareholder value. As other chapters in this book reveal, they sought to minimise their tax returns to the UK government by setting up various entities in tax havens. They encouraged hedge funds and private equity to engage in speculative activity by lending them capital, by trading complex derivative products with them, by facilitating certain trading strategies such as shorting shares (a common hedge fund tactic) and launching private equity takeover bids. In IPOs and privatisations they used their knowledge and power to ensure as far as possible that they maximised not just fees on the initial transaction but also profits in the secondary market. All of these activities were justified in terms of their role in making the financial markets more efficient.

Looked at from other perspectives, however, their impact was disastrous. They pushed other companies towards more short-term earnings strategies and away from investment in long-term growth. They engaged in complex tax avoidance schemes that robbed the UK Treasury of billions. They manipulated markets such as LIBOR for their own interests. They funded a massive and unsustainable asset price bubble, particularly in the housing market. They generated increasing inequalities by enabling managers to extract massive bonuses while encouraging other firms to reduce labour costs. The UK manufacturing sector shrank under this assault from the financial sector. SMEs barely got a look-in, as their business plans could never promise the rates of return that could be achieved by trading in the financial markets. Personal banking customers were subjected to high-pressure selling of unsuitable products, as banks sought to compensate for so-called 'free current account banking' by extracting fees and commissions from selling other financial products.

By the time of the crisis, these financial institutions had succeeded in making the United Kingdom a more unequal society, a more indebted society, a more regionally divided society, and a less productive economy. Yet when the crisis came, these same institutions went cap-in-hand to the state seeking rescue. Gradually the full extent of their actions and the consequences of those actions both before and after the crisis have become clearer.

In 2009 Lord Turner, chair of the Financial Services Authority in the United Kingdom, described much of the City's activities as 'socially useless', and questioned whether it had grown too large. He added that after a decade of excess 'beyond a socially reasonable size', the City had become 'swollen'. In a statement that reversed a decade of policy at the regulator, he said it was 'no longer one of his primary aims to promote the status of London as a global financial centre.'[1]

Although this idea that there needed to be a fundamental review of the role of financial services was supported by other commentators and academics, politicians in the United Kingdom and elsewhere were cautious about the consequences of such a critique, faced as they were by powerful interest groups lobbying for a return to 'business as usual' as quickly as possible. Propping up the banks and the financial sector more generally was seen as essential to avoiding a complete collapse of the economy. Yet such a propping-up placed huge pressure on state finances.

The recession following the crisis brought higher state expenditure on unemployment and other state benefits at the same time as tax revenues were falling, for exactly the same reasons. Keynesian arguments that this was a necessary counter-cyclical phase in order to ensure the economy did not collapse further failed to make much headway. In most European economies the dominance of neoliberal economic policy making pushed the need to reduce state expenditure in order to balance the books. As a result the crisis was reconstructed as a crisis of the state and state finances, requiring austerity for the bulk of the population. This approach quickened and became overwhelmingly dominant when the Eurozone crisis developed.[2]

In consequence, fundamental reform of the financial sector was downplayed. Instead fundamental reform was to occur in the role of the state, in particular reducing its overall level of expenditure and increasing the marketisation of services that had long been regarded as the responsibility of the state. This is not to say that there have not been reforms of the financial sector, but rather that they have been piecemeal and disconnected, trapped in negotiations between different states and regulatory authorities, and all the time subject to the massive lobbying influence of the financial sector.

Reforming the Banking Sector

As was shown in Chapter 7, the scale of the problem with the financial sector in the United Kingdom is huge. Given the fact that the financial crisis was caused by banks and that the problem of dealing with it on a global scale has proved so difficult, it is not too surprising that the result has been a series of piecemeal measures taken at a variety of levels:

national, European and global. But the agenda has been set by technical experts and the banks themselves. There has been minimal political and public involvement, and growing disillusion on the part of the public that they have anything to contribute.

There are a number of reforms that can begin to tackle this situation, but there is huge resistance to such steps. City defenders continually rehearse the dependence of the UK economy on the success of London as a financial centre, without considering the costs of that centrality, not only in the immediate period when the state had to rescue the City, but also over the longer term, when this power has undermined the competitiveness of British industry. It has also generated huge inequalities of personal wealth and income, and reinforced regional differences in the United Kingdom, which could lead to its break-up.

Overall it has made the United Kingdom dependent on its position as an easy, lightly regulated site for the funnelling of capital around the world. Such a position leaves the United Kingdom scrabbling to welcome all sorts of money, no matter what its origins and how it has been accumulated, so that its bankers and dealers can take their share of it. The UK state is supporting this no matter what the cost to its population. No wonder that population has become disillusioned with politics, when everything is made subservient to the needs of finance capital and the City of London. The result is a dangerous situation where extreme politics can flourish, with unknown consequences for the City as well as its opponents. If Scotland leaves the Union, or if the rump of the United Kingdom leaves the European Union following a UKIP-driven referendum campaign, can the City still survive?

Real reform of the City is essential for the future stability and development of the United Kingdom, whatever its future composition. There follow some of the reforms that need to be urgently addressed.

Controlling the Bonus Culture

The most high-profile issue for the public remains bankers' bonuses. High levels of incentives drove many bankers into making risky decisions while extracting from the system huge volumes of cash. This ended up creating wider inequalities within British society. In spite of these obvious consequences of an unregulated system, the UK government has backed away from statutory control, citing the need to maintain free labour markets so that 'global talent' can be attracted to and retained in London.

That same government is embarrassed and discomfited every time UK banks, including those with majority state ownership, announce their intention to provide bonuses to their staff. On an ad hoc basis ministers leap onto the populist bandwagon of criticising the banks. At the same time, however, the UK government is launching a legal challenge to the EU directive which limits the amount of bonus paid to a maximum of 100 per cent of base salary. This currently applies in the United Kingdom and in the branches of EU banks overseas. At a minimum, the cap proposed within the European Union should be supported and the government's effort to challenge it rejected.

The directive was designed to reduce the incentive for bankers to take on high risks, but the proposed rules have been watered down in response to lobbying from the financial community. Originally anyone earning over €500,000 (£425,000) would have been subject to a cap of 100 per cent of salary on their bonuses. The European Union then allowed this to be increased to a 2:1 ratio with explicit shareholder approval; and if the bonus is delivered long term (over three to five years), there is a further allowance. Now the European Banking Authority (EBA) has altered these rules, which came into force on 1 January 2014, so that banks are able to tell their domestic regulators that they are exempting staff up to €750,000 if they are not deemed to be taking or managing risks for the bank. Between €750,000 and up to €1 million the banks will have to seek approval from their regulator to exempt staff. Exemption for staff earning more than €1 million will need explicit EBA approval.

It has been estimated that 12,000 highly paid bankers, those earning €500,000 or more, will as a result be removed from the scope of the directive. EBA figures show that in 2012 more than 2,700 individuals in the City of London received more than €1 million, and that their average bonuses were 370 per cent of their salary.[3]

In spite of these changes, the UK government, backed by the Governor of the Bank of England, continues to oppose this measure on the grounds that it is detrimental to the banking sector in the City and its global competitiveness. This is an issue that has broad popular appeal. It also has the potential to have some limited impact on the behaviour of bankers. It is essential therefore that the arguments of the government against the cap continue to be challenged.

Structural Bank Reform

Some separation of banking functions must be actively pursued. The proposed long timescale for these reforms should not be allowed to mask their necessity. The New Deal response in the United States to the depression of the 1930s and the role that finance played in causing it was to reduce the size of the banks, first by not allowing cross-state banking, and second by not allowing the integration of retail with wholesale banking. The goal was to reduce the effect of any one bank failure by ensuring that it could not become so big as to threaten others. This was precisely the contagion effect which swept the financial markets in September/ October 2008 and practically brought down the whole system before governments intervened to provide cash.

In the United States, this structural issue has been taken seriously in what are called the Volcker rules, named after the former chair of the Federal Reserve. The rules prohibit banks from engaging in short-term proprietary trading in securities, derivatives, commodity futures and options, as well as limiting their exposure in hedge funds and private equity to around a 3 per cent ownership stake. The rules are effective from 1 April 2014, while the period during which banks have to conform has been extended to July 2015.

In theory, the goal is to shift high-risk proprietary trading out of the banking sector, where losses can contaminate the whole financial system, into specialist institutions that are not supported by the central bank and can be allowed to collapse. Banks will only be permitted to trade on behalf of clients, using client funds and not the bank's own capital, whether borrowed or not. Thus the banks will not sustain losses themselves. The impact of the Volcker rules in the United States is still unclear, as some exceptions have been made to the restriction on propri-etary trading and the monitoring and regulation of these activities has only just begun.

Goldman Sachs has been indicating that it wishes to continue to be active in proprietary trading, though quite how that will work is unclear. Some of its main rivals, such as JP Morgan Chase and Morgan Stanley, are shrinking this side of their business, a process reflected in the fact that a number of well-known traders have moved from these banks into hedge funds where they can continue with proprietary trading. The Volcker rules might be effective in reducing possible contamination effects inside large financial institutions, but they are not designed to stop high-risk activity in itself, since it will continue in the shadow banking sector of hedge funds.

In the European Union, the Liikanen Commission has produced a series of recommendations, including the mandatory separation of proprietary trading and other high-risk trading strategies from retail banking.[4] Its report was immediately attacked by the financial sector, and it was not until January 2014 that it resurfaced as a set of proposals from the European Commission, including banning proprietary trading of some financial instruments and ring-fencing other high-risk trading activities inside subsidiaries with their own specific capital requirements. The proprietary trading ban would apply as of 1 January 2017, and the effective separation of other trading activities would apply as of 1 July 2018.

In the United Kingdom the central recommendation of the Independent Commission on Banking was that a protective firewall should be put around the UK retail banking operations of big universal banks, such as HSBC, Barclays and Royal Bank of Scotland.[5] Customers' deposits, business lending and the transmission of money would be ring-fenced in new subsidiaries within the universal banks, endowed with increased capital resources to protect against losses. This has been broadly accepted by the government, though there are still details to be worked on, and implementation is not expected until 2019.

The key issue is whether ring-fencing within a single corporate group can actually work. Unlike the US proposal which is designed to separate the different forms of banking organisationally, with low-risk deposit, lending and money transmission in one set of entities and high-risk proprietary trading in another set, the approach in the United Kingdom and to a lesser extent the European Union appears to be to create a potentially unstable hybrid.

As we have already stated, these measures are not intended to reduce speculation and risk-taking in the financial markets. Indeed, they will push this out of the more tightly regulated sector into the shadow banking sector. Whether the major banks can be completely insulated from this sector in the event of a crash on the scale of 2007–09 is unclear. Also given how long it is going to take the United States, the European Union and the United Kingdom to work out what counts as proprietary trading, what exclusions might exist, what arrangements can be made to ring-fence high-risk activities that remain within the banks, as well as how each regulatory authority will deal with banks that are cross-national in scope and therefore subject to different regulatory regimes, we must remain cautious about whether this is going to have much impact on speculation and trading in the next few years. The longer the system struggles on without a second major crash, the less inclined politicians will be to insist on rigorous separations, and the more effective will be the banking lobby in trying to reduce the impact of these proposals. Politicians need to show stronger resolve, to communicate more clearly why structural reform is necessary, and to speed up their actions if anything is to be achieved.

Increasing Reserves

Bank regulators need to insist on high levels of reserve and lower leverage ratios, and not to allow the current proposals to be further diluted. It is doubtful whether higher reserves would have been sufficient to cope with the 2007–09 financial crisis. Nevertheless there needs to be a fundamental reorientation away from the idea that reserves should be minimised, because they are unnecessary and because they reduce returns to shareholders. In the immediate aftermath of the financial crisis, bank regulators in national jurisdictions and in the Basel Banking Committee agreed to push for higher reserves, but banks have fought long and hard to reduce the strictness of the rules.[6] It is now expected that banks will have to report their leverage ratios from 2015 onwards, and regulators intend to force them to have a ratio of at least 3 per cent, starting in 2018. But there is as yet no binding commitment.

Regulating OTC Markets

The regulation of OTC markets must be carried through, and ways found to reduce speculation by increasing the costs of entering and acting in the market. One of the main magnifiers of the crash in 2007–09 was the existence of OTC markets. This was recognised by the G20 at the London summit in 2009. Since then there have been moves to put these transactions onto regulated markets and central clearing houses. In this way, banks trading on the markets would have to put up collateral which would be used in the case of any counterparty reneging on its contract. This would in theory control the contagion effects which spread through the system in 2008. However, there are multiple complexities involved in this relating to different jurisdictions (such as the United States, the United Kingdom and the European Union), with different private platforms being authorised that have different operating rules and different periods of implementation.[7]

Derivatives markets in themselves have provided a range of useful functions by allowing actors to shift risk or to price it into their business plans. Where these markets have been on regulated exchanges, the counterparties have been required to provide collateral and to deal in products that are monitored and authorised by the exchange authority. In cases of counterparty failure, the overall risk remains limited and final losses are absorbed by the exchange. OTC activity has been very different, with bilateral trades that lack transparency and with risk management limited to the two counterparties.

Initially after the crisis it seemed possible that OTC activity would be banned altogether, but this has been a highly profitable activity for many banks, at least up to the financial crash, and the financial sector lobbied hard against forcing all derivatives onto regulated exchanges. As a result, there has now emerged a complicated structure within which contracts can remain bilateral but with central clearing houses that monitor and track deals as well as keeping tighter reins on collateral. Once again the regulators have accepted the arguments of the financial sector that the expansion of derivatives contracts in itself should not be regulated, even though this creates a vast speculative machine with the potential for huge losses and huge gains. Instead the regulators are aiming to limit the contagion consequences of this process, so that if one counterparty fails in a big way it does not have knock-on effects on other parts of the sector. Whether they have achieved this is still unclear, but what is clear is that they have done nothing to take speculation and risk out of the system.

Slowing Down the Markets with a Tobin Tax

One proposal which has been put forward that might reduce speculative activity is the Tobin tax. This idea was developed in 1971 by James Tobin, winner of the Nobel Prize for Economics. Tobin's original proposal was a tax on all foreign exchange transactions. Even if the tax were only at 0.5 per cent (which has been the figure generally quoted), this would have an effect on incentives to engage in currency speculation, as profits tend to be low in relative terms unless there is a currency crisis, and only become significant because of the scale of the amounts traded.

Tobin's idea was revived by the Asian financial crisis in 1997, in which currency movement and currency speculation played a significant role in the collapse of South Korea and other East Asian economies. Tobin's ideas have subsequently been extended to the idea of a general financial transaction tax applicable to trading in equities, fixed-income trading and derivatives. Tobin himself distanced his initial ideas from what he took to be its espousal by anti-globalisation social movements. Nevertheless the debate has continued, and has revived again in the light of the financial boom and then crash of the 2000s.

The argument in favour of a transaction tax are that it reduces incentives to trade and thereby brings down volatility in the markets. If it had not been so easy to buy CDOs or other complex financial products, because there was a tax on each transaction, perhaps the speculative bubble would not have inflated quite so quickly and so far.

The Tobin tax is of course opposed by the financial sector, ostensibly on the grounds that it would reduce the efficiency of the market. There have also been criticisms aimed at how the tax can be collected, and what it is to be used for. In September 2011 the European Commission proposed the introduction of a financial transaction tax (EU FTT) within the 27 member states of the European Union by 2014. Its structure was heavily influenced by debates over the Tobin tax. The tax would be imposed on financial transactions between financial institutions charging 0.1 per cent against the exchange of shares and bonds, and 0.01 per cent on derivative contracts. According to the European Commission it could raise €57 billion every year, of which around €10 billion (£8.4 billion) would go to the United Kingdom, which hosts Europe's biggest financial centre. The regulations would be implemented in such a way as to make it impossible to avoid the tax by moving offshore.

In spite of opposition from non-Eurozone EU countries, particularly the United Kingdom and Sweden, a group of eleven states, including France and Germany, have been pursuing the proposal. It was approved in the European Parliament in December 2012 and by the Council of the European Union in January 2013. The formal agreement on the details of the EU FTT still needs to be decided upon and approved by the European Parliament.

In February 2014, France and Germany pledged to reach a deal on the tax by May, even in the face of heated opposition from employers' associations within their own countries and the financial markets more generally. According to the *Financial Times*,[8] most countries backing the FTT in principle have deep reservations about it in its most ambitious form, and officials have struggled to agree on what a scaled-back version should look like. As a result discussion is converging around a stamp duty on equities and equity derivatives as a first step which could be expanded later. However this would raise little or no revenue for smaller Eurozone countries, and more importantly, Paris and Berlin remain at odds over how ambitious and automatic the second phase of the tax should be.

In the United Kingdom, opinion polls indicate that two-thirds of British people are in favour of some form of FTT. Organisations such as Oxfam have championed the idea, and War on Want has campaigned for what it terms a Robin Hood tax, based on the Tobin idea. Unfortunately in 2011, Ed Balls, the shadow chancellor, rejected the idea of a Tobin tax unless it was agreed globally. Given the strong resistance in the United States, this is unlikely.

For the Labour Party to give up on this popular and practical proposal, which is on its way to fruition in the Eurozone, is short-sighted, and indicates a continued failure to learn the lesson of the 2000s that it will gain nothing by cosying up to the City. Pressure to support the implementation of a Tobin tax in the eleven Eurozone countries would help build the case in the United Kingdom. At present, the opposition of David Cameron and George Osborne to the EU FTT and to the Tobin tax more generally is costing them little, even though their stand is unpopular, because the opposition parties are failing to grasp the advantages of the policy.

The Problem of Short-Termism

The problem of short-termism in major UK companies cannot be tackled without radically reforming the rules of the Stock Exchange. An essential aspect of the banking system has been its relationship to the stock market. The primary criticism of the financial system has been that its buying and selling of shares has nothing to do with the productive activity of companies, and is instead increasingly focused on maximising opportunities for quick gains as prices rise and fall. By engaging in this activity, the financial sector makes it very problematic for industrial firms to plan anything over the long term. Instead they are driven towards maximising shareholder value in the short term and becoming focused on their financial performance to the exclusion of all else.[9]

In the United Kingdom, this debate has been ongoing for some time. The financial crisis opened it up further because it was obvious that banks were little concerned about their corporate customers, either those operating on the London Stock Exchange or SMEs looking to borrow.[10] Even when the coalition government set targets for lending to small businesses by those banks that were predominantly owned by the state, the banks failed to meet them. The banks justified this in terms of lack of appropriate proposals. Essentially what they meant was that they were unwilling to risk money in the uncertainties of productive ventures when they could use that same money to make money in the financial markets.

In 2011 the government asked the economist John Kay to investigate the UK equity markets and the degree to which they were serving the interests of British industry.[11] Kay's conclusions strongly reinforced the argument that there was a problem of short-termism driven by the interests of the financial institutions in making money from quick deals and turnovers in the markets rather than investing in corporate businesses for the long term. Kay's recommendations were limited to issues such as more collective action by institutional shareholders via the establishment of an investors' forum, better disclosure of costs in the investment chain, transparency and fairness around the lending of securities, and better alignment between pay and long-term performance for company directors and asset managers. In other words Kay remained resolutely within the general consensus, which is focused on agency theory and issues of alignment to resolve the problems.

There is still strenuous opposition to more radical solutions such as the Tobin tax to reduce the incentive to churn continuously, as discussed above, or looking again at ways to control short-selling, a measure that was introduced in 'emergencies' but is now seen as an essential practice all the time. It allows hedge funds and others to pull down share prices. One option is to limit the voting rights of investors who have shorted shares and lent them to others, or have not held title for a minimum period of time to show commitment to the firm.

Tax reforms to reduce the advantages of private equity predators have also not been developed for fear of alienating other parts of the City. The Labour Party remains reluctant to engage too deeply in these discussions for fear of providing further ammunition to its enemies about its 'socialist' goals. It tentatively offers a state development bank as a source of strategic lending, while still concurring with efforts to return Lloyds and RBS to the private sector so long as competition 'on the high street' can be improved. This would be too little, and does not tackle the problems at their root.

Reforming a Failed Financial System

In conclusion, the financial system in the United Kingdom has failed. It has been given numerous chances to reform itself and has consistently not done so. Where governments have set up regulators, the industry has worked hard to make sure that its own interests become dominant inside the regulator so that it can continue to develop with a 'light touch' and with relative freedom from public scrutiny. The financial crisis of 2007–09 and events since then have served only to emphasise that the self-interest at the heart of this system will not be wished away by the pious words of chief executives suddenly converted to corporate social responsibility in the world of banking. That kind of talk is simply the latest effort to blunt real and essential reforms.

To repeat, what we believe is needed are:

- measures to set specific limits on bankers' bonuses
- measures to limit the proprietary trading activities of large banks
- measures to reduce and monitor speculative OTC trading

- measures to increase reserves and reduce leverage in financial institutions
- the imposition of financial transaction taxes and other measures to reduce short-term investment.

All these have all been brought forward and discussed over the last few years in various arenas. Every step of the way they have been opposed by the powerful financial lobby, generally supported in the United Kingdom by the coalition government. There is much popular opposition to the government's approach, particularly on the more visible issues of bankers' bonuses and the Tobin tax. This offers the basis for a more wide-ranging critique of the financial sector and its malign influence.

The Labour Party continues to hesitate in the face of the power of the City, meaning that campaigns continue to be disconnected and piecemeal. Bodies like Oxfam and War on Want can be successful in raising awareness, as can be more spontaneous activism such as the Occupy Movement. However, a much more powerful opposition can be built by the left in the United Kingdom joining in with the forces in the European Union that are struggling to constrain and regulate finance.

For the Labour Party, fear of the City, and fear of being associated too strongly with the European Union at a time when the future of the United Kingdom in the European Union is being placed in jeopardy by the politics of the Tory Party, are militating against such potentially productive alliances. The result is that the financial lobby in the United Kingdom continues to dictate its own terms, even after it has come so close to destroying the whole economy.

13

Small and Locally Based Alternatives

Corporations are not the only way in which people, production and markets can be organised. Previous chapters have concentrated on the problems with corporations, and documented some of the ways in which their power might be curbed and they could be made more socially responsible. If we unpick some of the decisions that have allowed unlimited incorporation, and decide to organise ourselves in different ways, the world of corporations is revealed as only one option out of many. This chapter suggests and recommends a different agenda, by exploring some of the other ways in which we might organise our businesses in a world beyond predatory capitalism.

To simplify matters considerably, there is one big problem with corporate forms of organisation, and that is their scale. Business enterprises do not have to be large to have a corporate form, but many of the most powerful of them are bigger than states and operate on a global scale. This is because they are addicted to growth, being based on economic models which assume that maintaining a steady state means stagnation and ultimately decline. Growth for them means that as the size of the cake increases almost everyone can enjoy a crumb or two more, so soothing potential conflicts over gross inequalities of distribution and control. The sheer size of the biggest corporations means that they do not behave like most human beings.

In the corporate world ideas about responsibility, care for and even recognition of others are not really relevant in other than rhetorical ways, despite the frantic frequency with which they are used. This characteristic of most corporations means that they tend to be forms of organisation which exhibit what Bakan calls 'sociopathic' behaviour, because they have little meaningful accountability to anyone other than shareholders.[1] This is what they believe they are required to do – to be machines that maximise profitability and externalise costs – and the fact that many of them operate in many different jurisdictions makes this strategy much easier to carry out.

This is not the only problem with the corporate form. Questions of regulation, ownership and management also matter, but it is a sensible opening for a discussion of alternatives.

Simply proposing organisational alternatives to corporations is not enough. Questions of corporate scale, structure and governance are not the only issues. There is a wider capitalist context to consider. Any organisation is embedded in a wider political economy. Though this is an obvious point, drawing attention to it should not be taken as a counsel of despair, an admission that nothing can ever really change. To say that organisations are embedded in an economy is also to say that they constitute that economy, because 'the economy' does not exist separately from the institutions which make it up.[2] If this is accepted, changing the structure and governance of business will change the economy, and as the economy changes, so too will businesses have to change. Organisation and environment are in a dynamic, interdependent and co-productive relationship, not a causal one. Lots of small changes by lots of small organisations could make life sufficiently uncomfortable for the leviathans currently trampling around the globe that they would have to evolve and change, or face decline.

So our analysis begins by thinking about the relationship between responsibility and scale, between the capacity to see and be seen, and the kind of actions that are then likely. This leads us to suggest smallness and locality as central principles of any alternative economy and organisation. This is followed by sections on alternative means of finance and exchange, and of management and ownership, again stressing the ways in which a wide variety of alternatives are feasible. The currently dominant forms of organising must be seen as a political choice, not the inevitable result of unavoidable market forces.

Responsibility and Scale

In ethical philosophy, there is a persistent concern to understand what sorts of conditions produce sympathy, empathy and responsibility. From Adam Smith to Emmanuel Levinas, many philosophers have concluded that distance is bad for ethics, and that having face-to-face relationships with others is the best way to cultivate dense ties that bind, and so foster human flourishing and preserve ecologies. The same has been said by many sociologists, explaining concepts like community, anomie and bureaucracy as effects of proximity or its lack. Forms of organisation and technology that prevent us from seeing others – whether they are management hierarchies, extermination camps or weaponised drones – can often lead ordinary people to do things that they would otherwise feel ashamed of.

Business organisations are a case in point. Business ethics texts are full of examples of corporate action which was justified at the time in the name of the organisation, and of the terrible effects on employees, customers, citizens or the environment of following the orders of management. It is easier to justify dubious action if you cannot see the faces of those that you hurt, easier to dismiss others if they can be lumped together as members of a category that things have to be done to.

This often means that the ethics of business differ from the sort of ethics we might use when evaluating actions carried out by people. It is assumed that 'business ethics' and 'corporate responsibility' are not the same sorts of thing as 'personal ethics' or 'personal responsibility'. This is precisely why scale is important, because otherwise we might be misled into believing that businesses could have ethics or responsibility in the same way that we might understand people to be ethical. It is an easy mistake to make, but a dangerous one because it encourages us to believe that corporations can change if 'they' want to. However since corporate logic encourages 'sociopathic' behaviour, and normalises and rewards it, they cannot. Corporations may go through the motions, and they may pull back from the most injurious behaviour to avoid excessive reputational damage, but if we want corporations to behave better than they do, it is not enough to get them to issue mission statements on ethics and responsibility. That is because, in their practical implementation, these declarations will not mean what we think or want them to mean. Instead, they will mean what corporations want us to mean by them.

Corporations will favour varieties of 'greenwashing', showing trees on the front of annual reports, rather than placing ecological preservation and renewal above shareholder value. We should not expect corporations to change in any significant or substantial way, so they will either need to be regulated by states, pressured by citizens or replaced by different kinds of organisation.

Smaller organisations are not perfect, and it is important not to romanticise them, but they can do less damage than larger ones. *Small is Beautiful*, the title of a 1973 book by the economist Ernst Schumacher, was essentially a series of arguments about a preference for forms of organisation and technology created on a human scale.[3] 'Gigantism' – whether of corporations, economies or technologies – according to Schumacher, dehumanises work and workers and produces forms of behaviour that damage the planet. Small, human-scale forms of social and material technology are better because they use fewer resources, have shorter supply chains, and cause less harm if they go wrong. Positively, people involved in smaller-scale organising are more likely to have meaningful responsibilities to suppliers, employees, customers and the environment.

These arguments are easy enough to make, and they have often been made. Yet the standard understanding of such matters among policy makers, business people and economists is the reverse. Scale is presumed to be good because it allows for efficiencies of various kinds. When they are investigated, these 'efficiencies' rely on reducing costs through pressure on suppliers by monopolistic practices, by automation which reduces employment, by labour intensification which increases productivity, by attacks on worker organisation, by moving employment to cheaper labour markets, or on evading regulation or taxes through offshoring business structures. In other words, achieving 'economies of scale' is usually a euphemism for paying less to make something or provide a service, but maintaining the same, or preferably increasing, levels of profit.

Many alternatives to corporate systems are based on different scales of organisation, on an economy that operates at a different scale and scope. These can be summarised as forms of localisation which emphasise face-to-face exchange and are suspicious of long distances. Many of these tendencies can be seen in the 'slow food' movement which was established in Italy in the mid-1980s (www.slowfood.com). Growing out of anti-McDonald's protests, the movement has since expanded considerably, and the 'slow' prefix has been applied in many other contexts. Rather than accepting the globalisation of 'fast food', there is an emphasis on rescuing and developing local culinary traditions and foods for each eco-region. This has involved creating grassroots organisations, establishing seed banks, protecting small farms and producers, as well as educating people and lobbying about the health and environmental problems with food gigantism and factory farming.

It is worth pausing here to note that this 'slow' and localised strategy involves two forms of resistance. One is the resistance to the incursions of large corporations and an encouragement of small businesses. The other is a resistance to the marketing that sells the idea that we can eat anything we want, whenever we want. In a sense this is a movement which is against a particular version of 'choice'. Like many alternatives to corporate dominion, it could be called 'protectionist', but it is so in a positive sense. It protects something from destruction by a set of pressures and associated interests that seek the replacement of local organisations, practices and tastes with the heavily marketed and standardised supplies of mega-corporations in a global market with no boundaries.

This emphasis on protection can be understood in terms of arguments about freedom. When we speak of being free, we usually mean 'free to', in the sense of being free to be able to exercise choices about who to vote for, what to buy, what to eat and so on. This is precisely the idea of liberty that we are often encouraged to imagine as the pre-eminent principle around which our lives should be organised within a consumer society. It is also the concept that those who market corporate values present as an aspiration that can be met only if we use their products and services.

A moment's thought allows us to see that 'freedom to' is only possible if we also experience 'freedom from'. As the political philosopher Isaiah Berlin put it, 'positive' and 'negative' liberty are not the same things, even if they appear to be aimed at the same goals.[4] The individual freedom to be who we want to be rests on being free from hunger, dislocation, violence and so on, goals which can only be pursued collectively. If we apply this to the corporate economy, we can ask for 'freedom from' having small businesses destroyed by supermarkets, internet warehouses and McFood chains, or having mutual housing associations absorbed by big banks, or having the environment degraded by profitable corporate activities.

A good example is the campaigns against the planning applications for supermarkets in many towns in the United Kingdom. The campaigners have produced well-documented evidence on everything from the effects on transport patterns to the viability of town centres (see www.tescopoly. org), although because of the nature of the UK planning system, they are often not successful in preventing the applications from being approved. This freedom from corporate predation is not usually a version of freedom that is celebrated, but it lies at the basis of many of the best alternatives to corporate capitalism.

There are a variety of ways in which this emphasis on scale and localism has been understood. In terms of communities themselves, the 'transition towns' movement which began in Kinsale in Ireland and Totnes in Devon (www.transitionnetwork.org) started with the idea of an 'energy descent plan' towards a zero-carbon economy. It has since become an umbrella for a series of ways of understanding community in dense and fruitful ways. For example, the idea of 'permaculture' (www.permaculture.org.uk) which underlay these early transition movements suggests exploring sustainable production methods for food and raw materials which mimic natural systems. It also implies forms of human organisation that are based on forms of co-operation and interdependence, such as eco-villages (http://gen.ecovillage.org) and community-supported agriculture (www.soilassociation.org).

A similar concept, but at a larger scale, is the idea of 'bio-regionalism'. This is based on a critique both of gigantic states as forms of governance and of the sort of global homogeneity in nature and culture which corporations seek to produce and sell (www.bioregional.com). For protagonists of these ideas, the injunction to think on a human scale is one that applies to all forms of human organisation. It presses us towards small-state, city-state or garden city forms of political organisation, and away from the idea that 'growth' is a good in itself. Indeed, growth is often understood by proponents of small alternatives as a pathology, since it is seen to sever ties and replace meaningful responsibilities with the extraction of value to the benefit of others, who are often located far away in distant capital cities.

Decroissance is a term coined by French radical economists to refer to and call for economic downscaling, or 'degrowth' as it has been translated into English (www.degrowth.eu). The term was first used by the economist Nicholas Georgescu-Roegen,[5] and has since been important in radical political debates about alternative economic systems in France, notably in a monthly magazine entitled *La Decroissance* (www.decroissance. org). The idea of degrowth was put forward to free economic thinking from the 'tyranny of growth', pointing out that growth and ever-increasing consumption are unsustainable both socially and ecologically.

Current measures of growth such as gross national product (GNP) only take into account the production and sale of commodified goods and services, ignoring its impacts, often negative, on other matters that we might value: justice, equality, democracy, quality of life, social relations, human health and the health of ecosystems. Logically, the solution to social and ecological problems is not to make growth greener or more socially equitable, but rather to challenge the very principle of growth. The answer is to produce and consume less, especially in the Global North. Proponents of degrowth want to encourage political debates on the collective choices facing societies, and on alternative models of social and economic organisation; for example by questioning our relationship to work and calling for much-reduced working hours. The hectic world of the contemporary corporation might then seem a long way away.

Alternative Money and Exchange

Drawing a picture of a new economy like this might seem to be utopian, in the sense that we have no road map for getting from the world of corporations which we presently inhabit, to the Arcadian future of small, local and degrowing enterprises. This is true, if we imagine the world of corporations to be dominant and seamless, but the work of quite a few social scientists suggests that this is far from the truth. Colin Williams has convincingly demonstrated just how much labour and exchange is not commodified, and has nothing to do with corporations.[6] Think of all the work that gets done for free, voluntarily, on the black market, or as part of some sort of exchange of services or hospitality within networks of family, kin, neighbourhood and community. As J. K. Gibson-Graham has argued, it is important to put capitalism and corporations in their place, and to observe that there are many examples of work and exchange that take place perfectly effectively without them.[7]

Corporations are big and noisy creatures, and it is easy to imagine that they are dominant because they spend a great deal of money ensuring that we know that they exist. Yet if we look a little more carefully below the tip of the iceberg we can see neighbourhood bakeries and cash-in-hand work, or hairdressers running their own businesses, farmers markets, allotments, credit unions and building societies. All these are ordinary enough. Yet if we add up the 99 per cent of organisations in any developed economy which are classed as SMEs with less than 100 employees, the vast majority of which have less than ten employees, then corporations begin to look a little less ubiquitous, and perhaps even a little more fragile.

The point is that the localised and responsible alternatives described above are actually not as far away as we might think. Encouraging them to multiply might quickly expand an economy that already exists but is invisible to followers of the Dow-Jones and the FTSE. So what sorts of practices might help to encourage a post-corporate world?

Take, for example, a local exchange and trading Scheme (LETS) (www.lets-linkup.com). A LETS is created where a group of people form an association and create a local unit of exchange. Members then list their offers of, and requests for, goods and services, priced in a local unit of currency, which might be an hour of labour, or some sort of virtual or material currency. Individuals decide what they want to trade, who they want to trade with, and how much trade they wish to engage in. The price is agreed between the buyer and seller, and the association keeps a record of the transactions. The level of LETS units exchanged is thus entirely dependent upon the extent of trading undertaken, and you don't need to earn money before you can spend it. LETS are formal associations for pursuing economically oriented collective self-help based on not-for-profit and mutual principles. They operate in order to fill the gaps existing in the provision of goods and services to meet needs and wants that are fulfilled neither by the private or public sectors nor by informal networks.

A similar model is the complementary or community currency, usually arranged in order to ensure that economic transactions stay within particular localities (http://complementarycurrency.org). By making decisions about which businesses are included and which are excluded, the organisers can establish a territory within which a local currency is circulated, encouraging purchasing and trading practices within that area. The association can also build different rules into its currency, such as depreciation rates to prevent hoarding and encourage trade or exchange rates with national currencies.[8] Crucially this is a form of economic arrangement that locks corporations out by adding some friction to flows of exchange. It is another form of 'protectionism', as it attempts to ensure that one economy is not commensurable with another, and that its assets and labour cannot be priced in terms that are useful to the other party. This is a way of refusing to trade on the terms established by corporations, for which 'the free market' is a necessary condition for their own advantage and 'trade barriers' are there to be taken down.

Reviving the Mutuals

LETS and complementary currencies are not as novel or impractical as it might seem. They operate in a similar way to the friendly societies, sick clubs, building clubs and societies, and savings and loans associations which were established in the early years of the industrial revolution in the countries of the Global North. Given that many citizens lacked kinship networks in the localities they inhabited and that kinship networks were the principal source of mutual aid, these local financial institutions provided those without such a local network with a substitute network of mutual aid.

In the United Kingdom, the building society movement was a good example of the potential strength and long-term sustainability of this form of local financing, until the neoliberal 'deregulation' of the 1980s which decimated an established network of small locally named and based institutions. Many of them were absorbed into highly leveraged national and global institutions, most of which have subsequently collapsed or been rescued. Credit unions, which operate on a similar basis, still survive in many areas, but without active support and the removal of government-backed over-regulation and disincentives they too are at risk from the corporate banking system.

As with all the examples discussed so far, these mutual organisations illustrate the importance of a certain sort of intimacy as opposed to giganticism. Mutual institutions do not have shareholders who can expropriate profits elsewhere, as all the investors and borrowers become members rather than owners. Mutual financial institutions can operate at many levels, from large health insurance companies to small credit unions, but the underlying principle is the same: that only the people who contribute to and use the services of the organisation benefit from its operation. If a surplus is made, it is reinvested in the business or shared among members, and not dispersed as dividends to external shareholders. Other measures of the success of mutuals could include houses built, jobs secured, and investments in local amenities. The value of a local mutual bank or credit union might be measured not on its profits statement, to be read by speculators far away, but on whether it has lent money to keep a particular small business going.

Collective Responsibility and Employee Self-Management

The point of comparing mutuals and cooperatives with more freestanding alternatives like LETS and community currencies is to suggest that the problem of the corporation is only partly about 'the corporation' itself. Mutual building societies and cooperatives are all incorporated bodies, just like ordinary companies and multinational corporations, but they are structured and governed in an entirely different way. The real problem with commercial corporations is the assumptions that are commonly made about scale, growth, free trade, and profit and shareholder value. The dominant ways in which these questions are settled favours large limited liability organisations which are addicted to growth and hence require unlimited resources and markets.

The dominance of the contemporary corporation is a 'rational' response to this environment, but the leading corporations are also powerful agents in shaping the environment in ways that are advantageous to that domination. Corporate PR pays the cost of persistent and effective lobbying of states and global trading associations to alter laws and common understandings in order to ensure that they can do what they want, where they want, and generally without any form of personal liability.

The whole point of limited liability, as it has been legally defined over the last century, is the evasion, or at least the narrow restriction, of responsibility. Unlike partnerships, where partners suffer the full consequences of business failure as well as enjoy the success, in corporations the liability of executives, investors and speculators is limited to their stake in the enterprise. The forms of economy described above all involve the acceptance of some form of liability, and ensuring that decisions and their consequences are clear to those on whom they have an impact. This is not to say that conflicts of interest disappear, but that the issues that are being discussed are visible to those people they affect.

Questions of responsibility are most clearly at issue when we come to the question of who governs the corporation itself. If neoliberalism has established the contemporary macro-economic framework, then it is the ideology of *managerialism* that shapes its assumptions about organisational behaviour.[9] Managerialism can be summarised as the belief that organisations should be governed by a special class of people with distinctive skills and language, and that these people deserve higher levels of reward and status for engaging in this activity. University business schools have actively promoted this idea as a way to sell their courses, but it is also an ideology which has been central to the growth of the growing economic class, which comprises the large body of supervisors, overseers and bosses which has emerged to control complex productive processes and to act as agents of the owners.

Once again giganticism is important, as it has provided ideal conditions for the emergence of an allegedly expert cadre of labour for corporations whose activities and interests are clearly oriented towards the continuation of the corporate form. All organising needs coordination. The important question is whether a differentiated group of well-rewarded individuals with a commitment to shareholder value should undertake the design and control of others' work, or whether the workers themselves can play an effective part in the process.

Worker self-management (WSM) is the idea that those who produce value should control their workplaces, making decisions on what is produced, how it is produced and how the organisation is structured.[10] It is based upon the assumption that hierarchical forms of management and organisation are functionally unnecessary, politically undesirable, and can be replaced by democratic forms of decision making. WSM is usually organised through participatory or elected bodies including workers' councils, supervisory boards, and other forms for the encouragement of greater participation in the running of a workplace. Notable historical manifestations of this economic model include the emergence of worker collectives during the Spanish Civil War in the 1930s, the

Mondragon cooperatives in the Basque region of Spain, and recuperated factories in Argentina after the financial crisis. Successful examples of WSM have included factories, health care clinics, transportation services and publishing companies. They have involved many different arrangements for voting, meetings, consultation and decision making. This is not a rare and temporary phenomenon, but a long-standing alternative which can be dated back as far as mediaeval guilds.

WSM is not without its critics. Predictably managerialists argue that economic democracy is too slow, inefficient and unpredictable. Given the catalogue of global problems documented in earlier chapters which have been caused by managerially managed corporations, the slower forms of decision making suggested here might actually be preferable, particularly if they squeeze out the profit-led versions of organisational efficiency favoured by neoliberals. Meaningful democracy requires time for thought and discussion. WSM provides models for new forms of self-sustaining workplaces and communities based on participatory economics. It provides examples and skills for developing a new way of thinking about what it means to work.[11]

From the 1970s onwards many firms and management gurus responded to the massive waves of labour insurgency and unrest by focusing on ways to increase worker participation and involvement in production methods, and improvement of the quality of working life. These attempts, often described as empowerment or job enrichment, were often not efforts to create self-determining structures for workers, but rather methods for giving greater autonomy within a set structure determined by the firm, thereby excluding any opportunity for self-determination. The whole point of WSM, in contrast, is that decisions about the form of democracy are also taken by the workers. Power is not granted by management as a privilege, but assumed by workers as both a right and a sensible way to run their own workplaces.

Locally Based Co-operatives

The assumption of power means little unless it is based on some sort of common ownership. A more common and powerful alternative to the managerial corporation is the co-operative. These are organisations within which ownership and control rest with members rather than outside owners. In ideal terms, a co-operative is an autonomous association voluntarily joined to meet common economic, social, and cultural needs and aspirations through joint ownership and democratic control.

There are three main types: the consumer co-op, in which a group of people pool together their resources to buy quality food or other daily necessities in large quantities and sell to each other at low price; housing co-ops, in which property is bought or leased by the co-op and rented out to tenant members, who through their rents are able eventually to build up a share account that corresponds to the value of their house; and finally worker co-ops, as described above. Not all co-ops are worker managed. It is possible to have collective profit sharing without a very effective democracy, as in the case of the John Lewis Partnership. Yet there is generally an assumption that those who put in or 'invest' capital and labour will have some say in the way that those resources are used, both in the management of labour and in the determination of the objectives of the organisation. In other words, members of co-ops are not simply employees who must do as management commands.

According to the International Co-operative Alliance (www.ica.coop), co-ops should be based on a number of principles. First, they are voluntary organisations, open to all persons able to use their services and willing to accept the responsibilities of membership, without gender, social, racial, political or religious discrimination. Second, members actively participate in setting policies and making decisions as well as contributing to the capital of their co-operative. They usually receive limited compensation, if any, on the capital they subscribed; and decisions regarding the distribution of any surplus, whether to reinvest in the co-op, to raise employee pay, or to support education or community activities, are taken democratically. Co-ops are autonomous, self-help organisations controlled by members. If they raise funds from external sources, they do so on terms that ensure democratic control by members and maintain the co-operative's autonomy. Finally co-ops work for the sustainable development of their communities through funding approved by their members, and work with other co-ops to achieve the overall goals of the movement.

This is an idealistic picture of co-ops. As the recent history of the UK Co-operative Bank has shown, they can become large corporate bodies in which the ideals of co-operative control by members become increasingly difficult to maintain. Large corporate co-operatives are not invulnerable to stupidity, cronyism or corruption. No organisational form is perfect. Yet the whole point of the co-operative form is that it is well established and successful the world over.

In England in 2010 there were 4,784 co-ops with a turnover of £29.7 billion. The global figure is 1.4 million co-ops with nearly 1 billion members and over 3 billion people securing their livelihood through them.[12] Co-ops exist in every sector of the economy, and have been thriving for centuries, initially as a response to the establishment of monopolies of various kinds. It is in the early co-op movement that we again see connections with the alternative economic arrangements discussed above. Two centuries ago, in order to combat the poverty and exploitation inflicted by capitalism, the Welsh social reformer Robert Owen proposed the development of 'villages of co-operation', in which members of around a thousand people would pool resources to acquire land and capital that would enable them to live self-sufficiently, exchanging only among themselves on the basis of 'fair deals'. Owen's attempts at establishing new forms of workplace and community were predicated on the assumption that an alternative to early capitalism was going to require radical rethinking of all aspects of political economy and authority. Two hundred years later, and arguably in a period of late capitalism, it is no different.

Establishing the Post-Corporate Economy

In order to work towards a world no longer dominated by corporations, many things need to be altered. Some of them will involve states using their regulatory powers to prevent corporations doing some of the things described in this book. Any serious attempt to curb corporate power must involve legal reform supported by effective compliance and inspection regimes, but corporations can also be put in their place or displaced if states strongly encourage the birth and growth of smaller locally oriented and worker-owned organisations which can easily supply the food, the clothing and the other consumer goods currently supplied by corporations.

In a way, this policy involves no more than levelling the playing field so that the local bakery can compete with the supermarket down the road, and employee ownership can grow from its current position, in which it represents only 2 per cent of UK GDP. This will involve constructing planning and taxation regimes, and labour standards that are protectionist, in the positive sense of nurturing diversity by preventing the elimination of all these forms of small locally based alternatives by large national and multinational corporations.

There is something of a contradiction in this conclusion. This chapter started with praising smallness, yet we now seem to be saying that a larger form of organisation – the state – is required to do things to protect these fragile forms of localism. This points to something of a fissure between attempts to regulate markets by using governmental power, and a 'post-capitalist' world of small states, small business and mutualism. Each approach has its problems. The idea that the state might turn against the corporation is politically improbable, particularly since the large state and the large corporation are in lockstep. Each lobbies the other for jobs, taxes, tax breaks, incentives, contracts and political support. Even if their purposes might seem opposed, they each require what the other has. Even if they are well intentioned, politicians and policy makers have difficulties when corporations threaten to close factories, move research and development elsewhere, lodge legal challenges and lobby against them. So supporters of mutualism must not assume that multiplying the small is going to be easy. There is a shared addiction to growth – to maintain profits and to attract votes. Backed by the state, corporations have a long and ignoble record of using their deep pockets to put smaller competitors out of business by undercutting prices, cornering the supply of raw materials, and using aggressive marketing techniques. The café using locally sourced ingredients located next door to McDonald's is going to struggle to survive.

In practice both control by regulation and the multiplication of alternatives are probably going to be required in the short term to constrain corporate power. In the longer term, we might hope that a new economy develops, and that the alternatives discussed above begin to thrive in a context in which, as ecological and social crises deepen, people become increasingly disillusioned and even hostile to giganticism, managerialism and the dominance of shareholder value.

Praising smallness is really just a way of encouraging the taking of responsibility, of insisting on the embrace of liability and not its limitation. Forms of mutual finance and worker self-management are ways of ensuring that people are never forgotten, never reduced to categories and no longer subordinated to the logic of the market. By using new communications technology and federalist and networked structures, the 'will of the many' can actually manifest itself on fairly large scales.[13] Small can become larger, and the influence of different models of decision making, ownership and exchange can be illustrated at levels that force states and corporations to take notice. Smallness can be multiplied, and with growing numbers can become a real alternative.

But this is not all that needs to change. The very way in which we think about organising also needs to become more politicised. Consider the example of accounting. At the moment, business schools and professional associations teach a form of accounting, both management and financial, which makes monetary return on investment the dominant criterion of an organisation's success. This is what corporations want, as it allows managers to pay themselves what they wish and shareholders to be fed their dividends regardless of how they were extracted, but it has become a measure by which most other organisations are judged too. This is the so-called 'bottom line', the final reality check on all utopias, and the reminder that nothing can ever really change.

However, what if students and practitioners were taught a form of accounting in which many other forms of success might be judged: the creation and retention of jobs, the contribution to a local community, the protection of the natural environment, the encouragement of healthy eating, of technologies that do not have undesirable side-effects, and of social and educational initiatives? All of these criteria and many others seem to be entirely reasonable things to expect and demand of human organisations. These objectives are what may reasonably be required of organisations created by human beings, populated by human beings, and intended to facilitate human flourishing. The techniques of accounting need to be changed in order to recognise and encourage other, broader and more sustainable objectives.

Or think about technology. At the moment technological development is dominated by large corporations which design and produce pharmaceuticals, smart phones, cars, genetically modified seeds and much else, with almost no public discussion beforehand about the social effects of those technologies. If there are profits to be made, the technology will be released into the wild, because the presumption is that technological change is good. Consider the way in which the container ship and associated technologies have destroyed ports, manufacturing, employment and tax revenues across the globe. There was no discussion over whether shipping vast quantities of consumer goods across the ocean was a positive development, no sustained attempt to protect the local against the impact of exposure to a huge low-wage distant labour market, no serious policy attempt to decide whether the flow of cheap goods was necessary or desirable, no assessment of the effect of gigantic container ships on global warming. In contrast, amongst the Amish of Pennsylvania, there are community debates about the introduction of new technologies, assessments of what is likely to happen to 'us' if we all start using mobile phones and other inventions. Some of the most invasive of technologies are publicly debated in the Global North – the merits of genetically modified crops, genetic therapy and nuclear power are all hotly contested – but the majority are not. So, if a corporation sees a market opportunity in selling an internet-enabled fridge, it will do so, regardless of its social and environmental impact, good or bad.

Mainstream economists, business people and politicians claim that the only judgement of economic activity is 'the market', and that corporations, being creatures of the market, are best placed to decide on what they should or should not do. It is an argument embedded in our taxation systems, in business school education, and even in our assumptions about accounting and technology. At the moment we confront corporations as if they were a fact of nature, a kind of god that has always been with us and to which we need to prostrate, or at least accommodate, ourselves or risk annihilation. In order to confront them, it is important to remember that they only exist because we made them, just as we have established the markets to which corporations claim to be responding. The problem is that corporations have managed to make themselves appear natural and indispensable. We have been persuaded that the forms of order and exchange they represent are a result of inexorable processes, processes that are almost instinctually associated with ideas about evolution, competition, free choice and trickle-down justice. As a consequence, it appears that there is no alternative, that what exists is the one best way, and that we have arrived at the end of history.

In order to dispel such collective deception, it is vital to retain and nurture the understanding that organising is politics made durable. All forms of organisation represent political choices about how we wish to live, and how we wish to live with others. Over the millennia human beings have organised themselves in many different ways, and at many different levels of scale, with greater or lesser degrees of success. As soon as any powerful institution becomes dominant, its position is normalised and defended by those who have benefited, claiming a mandate for its continuation into the future. In our era the corporation claims the market as its justification, and continually asserts that people who do not understand markets do not understand 'the real world'. If we begin from that premise, we will never escape the cold logic of profit and loss, compete or die. The corporation and its giganticism will appropriate or crush everything in its path as it calculates its advantages on a global scale, because it has no responsibilities, no liabilities of the kind that small vulnerable human beings have.

To forestall and counteract the dystopia of the corporation, it is necessary to remind ourselves that human beings make human worlds. If we engage in forms of organising that keep human beings firmly in mind, then the many failings and pathologies of the corporation no longer look like inevitable collateral damage. Instead, the utopian schemes of those who want to build participatory economies, worker-managed firms, appropriate technologies and slow foods look like politics.[14] However, the corporation is also a form of politics, and once matters become political, then they are by definition open to change.

14

Towards New Corporate Forms

A premise of this book is that collective activity – involving productive forms of co-operation and coordination, rather than atomised actions undertaken by individuals or small groups – is of immeasurable value, as it enriches human existence in numerous directions – socially and spiritually as well as materially. The question is how this capacity can be harnessed effectively so that it supports human flourishing and creativity, rather than oppression and insecurity.

In Part I of this book, we identified a number of pathologies of the dominant form of modern corporation: the public limited company or PLC. We noted how PLCs have become instruments of social division and domination. Instead of harnessing corporate potential to contribute to common well-being, their managers seek to escape their social obligations – by evading the payment of taxes, by minimising their wider responsibilities, by lining the pockets of shareholders and executives at the expense of others who lose their jobs or experience a deterioration in their terms and conditions of employment or their pensions. In Part II, we have pointed to ways in which such pathologies may be addressed and counteracted. We have resisted the assumption that abuses of the corporate form are unavoidable by insisting that they can be reduced through regulation, even if it is impossible to eliminate them completely. And we have challenged the presumption that the limited liability corporation offers the only, or best, means of securing productive forms of co-operation and coordination, as the previous chapter on local and worker-managed organisations has demonstrated. In this chapter, we consider a number of larger corporate alternatives. But, first, we must recall the benefits and risks associated with limited liability as a basis for assessing the relevance and contribution of alternatives.

Corporation Ltd

The merit of limited liability, from the perspective of investors, is that their risk is restricted to the loss of the value of their shares. In contrast to the participants in the partnership form, investors in what we shall call Corporation Ltd escape liability for any debts or other obligations incurred by the company. Clearly, this makes investing much more financially attractive. The benefits of receiving dividends and capital gains, and the ease of selling shares on a secondary market where a balanced portfolio can be created, far outweigh any losses, which are usually comparatively modest, well-spread and temporary. The downside, in terms of stewardship of the business, is that there is little incentive for shareholders to have any direct involvement in, knowledge of or sense of responsibility for the company.

Unlike most members of a partnership or a family business, shareholders are absentee owners whose interest is comparatively detached and speculative. They seek to invest in whatever will produce a strong return. If they are not satisfied, the easiest option is to invest elsewhere. A second shortcoming is the tendency to privilege shareholders over other stakeholders – employees, suppliers, customers and local community members – in the creation of assets. It was the conversion of investment banks from partnerships into companies which greatly increased the likelihood that senior executives would participate, more or less knowingly, in reckless forms of risk taking because there was no direct personal liability for failure. The exclusive and rampant pursuit of shareholder value, in which executives participated through performance-related bonuses and stock options, has illustrated the pathological tendencies of Corporation Ltd. When inadequately regulated, Corporation Ltd is free to ignore any wider public interest. The problem is that these corporations, as PLCs, have become so dominant, nationally and globally, that other forms of ownership and governance have been marginalised, rendered invisible or refashioned in the PLC image.

Whatever a corporation produces – goods or services – requires the involvement of numerous other parties and resources. There are many stakeholders, and the corporation would cease to exist without their involvement. Among them are suppliers and customers as well as employees and members of a wider community. Through taxation, members of the community pay for the infrastructures for corporations to create and distribute their products, educate their employees, look after them when they are sick or retired, and provide numerous other services which they would otherwise be obliged to deliver.

There are other costs that corporations externalise to the community, such as the degradation of the environment, healthcare costs associated with poor working conditions, and the wider consumption of products that cause ill health, disorder and long-term disability. What these developments reflect is an institutionalised erosion, if not a denial, of any substantial and meaningful sense of stewardship or social responsibility. In effect, competition unconstrained by effective regulation creates a race to the bottom where everything is degraded in the pursuit of better value for money, as it is this that yields competitive advantage and thereby increases the value delivered to shareholders.

At the centre of Corporation Ltd and its commitment and subservience to market forces is a very weak sense of social responsibility. In terms of governance and accountability, the primary responsibility is assumed to be to shareholders, with minimal or merely instrumental concern for other stakeholders. Responsibility is, quite literally, limited. This one-dimensionality is reflected in the constitution of the boards of Corporation Ltd, on which there is minimal, if any, representation from stakeholders other than investors and executives. The prioritisation of shareholders and the associated pursuit of shareholder value persists despite the appointment of non-executive directors (NEDs), which is unsurprising as NEDs are routinely drawn from the business elite of executives and advisors, and very rarely from other constituencies. The boards of Corporation Ltd operate in a self-serving space from which the voices of other stakeholders are effectively excluded.

In this bubble, 'diversity' is, at best, conveniently defined as greater representation of women and perhaps of ethnic minorities, but these 'diverse' individuals are also generally drawn from the same elite pool of directors and advisors. United by a common belief in limited liability capitalism, as well as bonds of class and education, they let prevailing assumptions and practices go unchallenged. Faith in and dependence upon Corporation Ltd impedes the prospect that the priorities of senior executives will ever be challenged in the boardroom by sceptical or dissenting voices, at least not before there are undeniable signs of corporate crisis, reversible decline or eventual collapse.

The absence of sustained accountability to diverse stakeholders makes corporations vulnerable to 'group think' and an associated discounting of other more inclusive and democratic forms of governance and decision making. It also makes the guardians of corporations defensive with respect to decision making beyond the boardroom that directly affects their position – in terms of employment regulation, the provision of public services and the taxation revenues required for funding a collective state.

Beyond Corporation Ltd

A peculiarity of the British economy has recently been illuminated by the Ownership Commission:

> Britain has disproportionately more PLCs than other countries, so it has disproportionately smaller Small and Medium-Sized Enterprises (SMEs). For example, there is nothing to compare with the famous German *Mittelstand*. At the same time, the customer-owned mutual sector is small and employee ownership is less significant than elsewhere.[1]

There is nothing inevitable about this dominance of Corporation Ltd. Once upon a time the limited liability company did not exist, and its continuing existence is conditional upon political endorsement.[2] There is no functional requirement that forces human beings to organise in this way. As we have shown in Part I, the current situation reflects a series of historical and contemporary choices, a complex amalgam of power, law and economics which has granted Corporation Ltd great power over our lives.

PLCs can be powerful engines of growth. They have improved living standards but they are also highly vulnerable to pathologies. They are more likely to become profit-maximising machines which calculate that ignoring the law is a business risk that is well worth taking when the prospects of being found out are slight and distant, and when managing the appearance of social responsibility is sufficient for preserving corporate reputation amongst customers and with politicians. In short, there is scant legal or moral obligation upon PLCs to recognise or fulfil stewardship obligations, and there is every incentive to minimise them where this does not risk damaging reputation to the point of losing sales or contracts.

A disturbing feature of the dominance of Corporation Ltd is a tendency to regard this as the default form, thereby marginalising or displacing other possibilities, as discussed in Chapter 13. Instead of diversity – including family firms, partnerships, mutuals, employee-owned firms and state-owned businesses – there is effectively a corporate monoculture in which plurality is excluded, colonised or privatised. In this monoculture, where the playing field is tilted to benefit Corporation Ltd, it can prove difficult for other corporate forms, such as co-operatives, to enter, compete and prosper. The crisis and partial takeover of the Co-operative Bank in 2014, discussed below, is a telling example of the problems that can emerge when one form of organisation seeks to copy and compete with Corporation Ltd on its own terms.

In general, the alternatives to Corporation Ltd do not enjoy the benefits of such ready access to finance, the prospect of rapid expansion or the comparatively risk-free returns offered to investors. But neither do they carry the same risks of hostile takeovers and highly leveraged financing. They are usually far better rooted in local communities where attentiveness to, if not direct involvement from, a range of stakeholders is more integral to their business rather than a contrived add-on to it. There is a strong case for the active encouragement of a more diverse and resilient range of corporate forms which can offer a choice to various stakeholders – employees, consumers, suppliers and investors – with regard to where they work, what they consume, who they do business with, how they save, and so on. So what other organisational forms exist as alternatives to corporations?

Partnerships

In partnerships, the risks and rewards of running a business are shared among the partners, who are personally responsible for the debts incurred by the enterprise. Because partners are directly liable for the risks of business, there is very limited public accountability, even though other stakeholders – employees, suppliers, customers – may be adversely affected by their decision making. Since 2000 in the United Kingdom, there has been the option of creating a limited liability partnership (LLP) where there is greater public disclosure but the liability of partners is limited to the amount of capital that they personally contribute to the partnership.

Such partnerships are able to issue tradable shares as an additional source of funds, but they do not pay corporation tax. Instead any profits are treated as taxable income of each of the partners, whether or not the money is actually distributed. But the distribution of profits is confined to the partners, who unlike PLC executives cannot receive share-options. In this respect, LLPs are something of a halfway house between partnerships with unlimited liability, and Corporation Ltd. The partnership form can also be used more creatively to incorporate many partners, in which they become more comparable to employee-owned firms, which are discussed below.

Family Firms

Family-owned businesses differ from Corporation Ltd in respect of their ownership. Most are incorporated as private companies in which a majority stake is held by members of the founder's family, at least one of whom participates in the governance of the firm. The challenge for family firms, which are often but not always SMEs, is access to funding. Bigger family firms, such as JCB Excavators Ltd, can usually borrow at reasonable rates. But for smaller firms this can be difficult, and there is a need for encouragement in the form of tax relief for long-term funding, improving credit flows from banks and/or facilitation for the issue of bonds by larger private companies.

There is also an issue over longer-term survival of family firms as it is not always possible or desirable for them to be passed to the next generation. Without this continuity, there is then the prospect of a takeover or decline. In many cases the default option tends to be a version of Corporation Ltd: sale to a competitor or flotation on the stock market. An alternative that could be better promoted and explored is assistance for a buy-out by employees or other stakeholders, as discussed below.

Mutuals and Co-operatives

These organisational forms can be considered together because they depart quite radically, but in similar ways, from other economic organisations. They include housing associations as well as a variety of financial institutions, such as building societies, and also producer and consumer co-operatives. Their purpose is not to enrich or gratify individuals, whether family members or partners; nor are they the creations of the centralised power of the state. They are geared to the service of their members, and they directly involve those members in their governance as well as their ownership.

Typically, the assets of mutuals and co-operatives are more or less securely locked within them. But the demutualisation of many building societies during the 1980s and 1990s in the United Kingdom demonstrated how asset locks may be vulnerable to the attentions of determined 'carpetbaggers'. It is instructive that none of the demutualised building societies survived the financial crisis.

A further example of the dangers of ignoring the essential differences between mutual and co-operative forms of organisation was the ill-fated acquisition of the mutual Britannia Building Society by the Co-operative Bank in 2009. This was intended to create a 'super-mutual' which could compete effectively with major high street banks. The subsequent attempt, backed by the Treasury and regulators, to persuade the Co-operative Bank to take over hundreds of branches of Lloyds Bank was similarly motivated by a concern to foster competition by cutting unit costs through economies of scale, adopting the approach of bigger corporate banks. The crisis in the Co-operative Bank in 2014 has demonstrated that arguments on the basis of scale are not necessarily good ones, and that assumptions about the necessity for growth do not suit all organisations.

So the purpose of mutuals and co-operatives is to pool resources in a way that provides something that is otherwise beyond the reach of their members, and not simply to increase their wealth through the payment of dividends. This is because surpluses are more typically used to develop the business and provide long-term collective benefits.

To assist in entrenching this longer-term perspective and to avoid domination by wealthier members or by external lenders, they are normally governed under a system of one vote for each member. Board members are thus democratically chosen from the members who stand for election, or in some cases they are democratically selected from candidates who are nominated by the board. In this way, those elected to the board are directly accountable to the members, and so in principle are more trusted by them. As there are usually no external candidates, the limited management expertise on boards can be balanced against the absence of pressure from financial markets to be dynamic and innovative.

Mutuals and co-operatives usually lack access to major financial and equity markets. This can be a blessing when weathering financial crises, but can also be a disadvantage when competing against corporations that enjoy the benefit of aggressive, short-term discounting as well as economies of scale achieved through more rapid and capital-fuelled growth. However, return on capital employed is an inappropriate performance measure for mutuals and co-operatives, whose primary purpose is to serve their members. Delivering this is ultimately dependent upon their survival in the face of competition from Corporation Ltd.

This point was demonstrated when UK retail banks entered the mortgage market and rapidly acquired a substantial market share. Between 1987 and 1997, the share of mortgages held by banks increased from 3 per cent to over 30 per cent. This undoubtedly damaged the remaining building societies, meaning that they were generating lower surpluses. Generating these surpluses was important to ensure that mutuals and co-operatives invested in technology, and recruited, trained and retained staff who were capable of ensuring that they were 'competitive' with regard to what was provided to their members, as consumers and producers.

Finally, unless there is a watertight lock-in of assets, mutuals are vulnerable to votes for demutualisation, which permits current members to cash in on the current value of an organisation that may have been created through the labour of many generations.

Employee-Owned Firms

Employee ownership refers to firms in which employees have a controlling stake either through the ownership of shares or within a trust. This form must be distinguished from employee share-ownership schemes, in which staff collectively have a very small percentage of the total shares, and therefore little basis for control; and also from co-ownership schemes, where the stake owned by employees is less than 20 per cent. Unsurprisingly, it has been found that many recipients of employee share schemes sell them as soon as they can, and that take-up of employee share options tends to be limited to those with greater disposable income, and so compounds income inequality with equity inequality.

In firms that are majority owned by their employees, staff may personally own shares in the business or may own the firm indirectly through a trust. In share-based schemes, they might have either purchased the shares or been gifted them. In the trust-based form of organisation, employees do not risk their own capital. They are beneficial owners, identified as members or partners, but have no personal stake in the firm, as this is held in trust on their behalf. The financial benefit they derive is in the form of an annual bonus or equivalent (comparable to a dividend), and in addition they benefit from terms and conditions that may also be comparably favourable.

Employee ownership is normally accompanied by substantial representation at non-executive board level, and managers are ultimately accountable to the firm's owners, the employees. As Davies observes, exactly 'how profits and voice are distributed depends on the constitution that is being used; but the possibility of power and financial reward being retained by a minority at the very top becomes inconceivable'.[3]

Employee ownership is often the result of business succession, where owners welcome an employee buy-out or establish a trust-based form of employee ownership. In principle, some elements of the trust-based form are attractive, as there is less incentive for employees to sell their ownership rights. The John Lewis Partnership (JLP) in the UK retail sector is a leading example. JLP is not owned by a family or other shareholders, but has been established as a trust under which profits, after sensible investment, are shared out proportionally among all staff, known as its Partners. It was established in 1929 by the conversion of his controlling shares into the participatory trust by the previous owner, John Spedan

Lewis. It has an impressive record in both commercial and human terms. Surpluses are distributed as an annual bonus (normally around 15 per cent of salary) to the partners, in addition to gold-plated pensions and other benefits. All 91,000 permanent employees thus own John Lewis department stores, Waitrose supermarkets, an online and catalogue business, johnlewis.com, and a direct services company, Greenbee.com, with a turnover of £9.5 billion in 2013. It is a much quoted model, but one that was initially dependent on an act of generosity and foresight by a wealthy businessman eager to establish a form of ownership and governance that he termed 'responsible capitalism'.[4] The partners also have a strong voice, underwritten by a constitution, in the governance of the firm, although this does not include direct control over the appointment of senior executives.

Hybrid forms of employee ownership involving at least 50 per cent indirect ownership are also possible. In these, employees can purchase shares but may then risk loss of their investment as well as their employment if the firm fails. There is less risk for both the employee and the firm in this case because shares are not tradable in a way that can present financial demands and difficulties when staff divest themselves of shares and/or when the firm is exposed to acquisition.

Like mutuals, employee-owned firms raise funds from loans and earnings, as they lack access to external capital. But in general there is stronger engagement from staff, who are more committed and productive and less instrumental in their relation to the firm. So employee-owned business can deliver greater employment growth as well as increased productivity relative to Corporation Ltd, and can also be more resilient during economic down-turns. They are subject to taxation rules designed for PLCs. But they do not enjoy the same taxation reliefs, another sign of a playing field tilted in the direction of Corporation Ltd. The profits of employee-owned firms are taxed twice, first when they are paid into the trust and again when they are distributed to employees. Moreover, as financial and legal advisors are less familiar with and perhaps less positively disposed towards the employee-owned firm, this corporate form is less likely to be contemplated as an option when considering business succession or development.

State-Owned Businesses

The state ownership of business has declined in the Global North in recent decades as a consequence of neoliberal policies of privatisation, thereby compounding the monoculture of Corporation Ltd which restricts choices for employees, suppliers and consumers as well as investors. The wholly or partly state-owned companies that remain in the United Kingdom are held within the Shareholder Executive, in which their performance is kept under review and their suitability for part or full privatisation is assessed.

For example, the state owns Post Office Ltd through the Postal Services Holding Company Ltd, as well as a 30 per cent stake (at the time of writing) in Royal Mail plc, the delivery company. Since 2009, the state has also owned the East Coast train operating company, which is being run successfully and profitably, but is intended to be returned to private ownership in 2015, despite a public campaign to keep it in the public sector. In addition, and with considerable irony for those in favour of privatisation, since 2006 the state has held, through UK Financial Investment whose sole shareholder is the Treasury, very large stakes in failed (demutualised) building societies such as Bradford & Bingley and Northern Rock, and two major banks, RBS and Lloyds.

With few exceptions, such as Post Office Ltd, where a mutuality option, to be discussed below, has been contemplated, the default approach has been the privatisation of public assets. An alternative has been to establish public benefit corporations or 'trusts' in health and education, through which public assets, such as 'foundation' hospitals and 'academy' schools, become nominally managed by elected governors drawn from local communities. This accountability to local communities is presently under threat, as the Academies Act 2010 provides for only two parent governors, a considerable decrease on the previous regime. A similar picture is evident in the National Heath Service, where board members are:

> drawn from staff and the public, including patients, [who] elect (most) of the board of governors of the Foundation Trust (a minority are appointed by partner organisations). These in turn appoint the chair and non-executive directors. The board consists of the non-executive directors, the chief executive (appointed by the non-executive directors) and executive directors appointed by the chief executive There has been a steady decline in participation from both sections of the Foundation Trust electorate – staff and public.[5]

The responsibility of a trust is to manage certain assets free from direct state control but monitored by central government inspectors. Whether current arrangements are sufficiently accountable to their users is certainly questionable. But the idea is actually quite similar to early versions of corporate status, granted by the monarch to institutions such as monasteries and universities, which were deemed to provide a public good.

A more innovative alternative that has been adopted by some local authorities as a means of avoiding pressure to contract out some of their services is what may be called 'not-for-profit spin offs'. A good example is Greenwich Leisure Ltd, which was spun out of Greenwich Council in 1993 by the leisure centre manager, and has since flourished. It now employs over 6,000 people and runs over 100 leisure facilities across London. There was no overarching national policy framework for these early not-for-profit spin-offs, and they occurred at a time when local authorities were making cuts in spending. Within the stark choices of either privatisation or closure that became prevalent within local government in the early 1990s, these trailblazing, mutually led enterprises showed that innovation was possible. Working together with a growing number of ethical manufacturers and co-operative agencies, this first wave of spin-outs created what are now referred to as the social enterprise movement. Their success showed that there was and is a viable alternative to the binary public/private sector choice previously contemplated.[6]

Another hybrid organisational form involves shared service delivery between public and private sectors. The most common version is the public–private partnership (PPP). These were developed to provide an 'off-balance sheet' method of financing public assets and services, thereby avoiding an increase in public debt. The asset, such as a hospital or school, is typically developed through a 'special purpose vehicle' (SPV) in which the government may hold an equity share if it has invested in the project. The asset is then leased to the public sector by the SPV, which maintains it for the length of the contract in exchange for a regular contractual payment. There have, however, been serious criticisms of whether these arrangements provide value for money, not least since the long-term risk remains with the public sector.

Finally, there has been experimentation with 'spin-offs' from the public sector, where assets are transferred to and services are provided by employees. For example, Hull's City Health Care Partnership left the NHS following three years of preparation. NHS staff that transferred kept their pensions and terms and conditions, and the Partnership was guaranteed a three-year contract to provide services to the NHS.[7] This organisational form may increase the involvement and commitment of those participating in the organisation, but unless it is carefully constructed and maintained, like most of the examples in this section it is vulnerable to poor governance and weak public accountability. A significant challenge is that 'the process of spinning out public services is complex, as the transfer of assets like buildings and liabilities like pensions requires extensive legal support that often does not exist within the public sector'.[8] We return to this point later when considering the creation of employee ownership trusts.

Promoting Diversity

All these diverse forms of business organisation coexist within capitalist economies. They demonstrate that we do not need to accept a commitment to a Corporation Ltd monoculture in which shareholders become privileged as the primary stakeholders, with others – employees, customers, suppliers and others – being treated as bystanders whose critical contribution to the production of value and wealth is barely recognised.

At the heart of that culture is the misconception that legal ownership of a company share is the same as ownership of the company, and with it comes the right to control a complex set of social relationships that comprise and rely on the contributions of diverse stakeholders. To the extent that some disquiet is expressed about the pursuit of shareholder value as the dominant motivation, it is presumed that any possible shortcomings can be corrected by encouraging greater shareholder activism, or extending the scope of audits, or rewarding social responsibility. Nor do we need to accept the involvement of hedge funds and/or private equity funds that use forms of leveraged buy-out to acquire a majority controlling stake in organisations, as in the acquisition of Co-operative Bank bonds which were reduced to junk status and snapped up by Aurelius Capital Management and Silver Point Capital.[9]

We need to facilitate and promote other forms of economic organisation, such as community interest companies which invest their profits in social objectives. This direction of development has significant consequences for the quality of life, social cohesion and economic stability. What is evident from our consideration of 'alternative corporations' is the diversity of possible ownership and governance structures.

The structure of Corporation Ltd facilitates growth primarily as a means of increasing the private wealth of its shareholders. It also provides employment in addition to whatever goods and services it produces. So not everything that the corporation does is parasitic on the social good. It is an organisation that can and does create benefits for a range of stakeholders, such as the provision of pensions for others through institutional investment by pension fund managers. Community interest companies or social enterprises may mimic the structures of Corporation Ltd, but they distribute their profits primarily for public benefit rather than for the material gain of private or institutional shareholders.

What Corporation Ltd shares with forms that are most congruent with it – notably, partnerships and family firms as well as hedge funds and private equity firms – is an exclusion of most stakeholders from any meaningful involvement in its ownership and governance. Seductive elements of ownership may be accommodated by freely distributing, or allowing employees to purchase, a very small percentage of the total shares. Some degree of involvement in low-level forms of governance may also be incorporated in an effort to extract knowledge from employees and/or to strengthen employee commitment. But participation by employees in ownership and governance, except for senior executives who acquire substantial stock options, is almost always marginal.

This is clear from the refusal since the 1970s even to consider the merits of two-tier boards, where a supervisory board comprises elected representatives of employees as well as banks, and other stakeholders have real powers over major decisions. As explained in Chapter 11, this model is well established in German companies with an Aktiengesellschaft (AG) structure, and has recently been given a new lease of life in an official review.[10]

Admittedly the Foundation Trust model developed for hospitals, discussed above, incorporates a two-tier board in which a group drawn from a wider community of users and experts oversees the board of executives responsible for day-to-day operations. But we believe this mechanism could be much more widely employed. For corporations, the chief virtue of this approach is its capacity to challenge executive 'group think' by encouraging consideration of the concerns of a wider constituency of stakeholders, including workers and future generations, and more extended horizons than those typically contemplated by many shareholders.

Two-tier boards can serve to broaden the accountability of executives and connect employees more directly to strategic decision making within the firm. Substantial employee co-ownership is another way of strengthening this connection, as well as encouraging employees to take responsibility for the asset with which they are entrusted. In principle the democratic and economic benefits associated with alternative corporation structures in the form of two-tier boards or substantial employee ownership can be mutually reinforcing, although in practice this can prove challenging. At their centre is the issue of engagement, which, in addition to investment, is crucial for innovation, productivity and economic survival. It is clearly possible for an alternative corporation to do all this, as the example of the John Lewis Partnership, Tullis Russell, Scott Bader and many others demonstrates: 'dispersing ownership and governance rights throughout the firm creates a greater sense of legitimacy about the decisions that are taken'.[11]

Conversely, simply offering opt-in share ownership to staff does nothing to increase their involvement in or influence over corporate governance, and potentially exposes them to a double risk to their savings as well as their employment if the firm fails. Such schemes may be presented as a form of performance-related pay, but in the absence of mechanisms to make managers more accountable to the as-yet-unlocked capacities of employees, the link is tenuous.

Employee Part-Ownership

One route to large-scale employee ownership, as outlined above, is through the establishment of a trust with a controlling stake in the business. When the assets of the firm are not gifted to employees and are not directly purchased through an employee buy-out, they can be used to underpin financing as security for loans for the full or part transfer of ownership to a trust. Where the transfer is partial, financing can be supplemented by individual share ownership by either employees or other parties. The latter route may, however, compromise governance arrangements and processes if individual shareholders are able to accumulate sufficient shares to exert influence over the firm, and even mount a successful takeover. If shares are restricted to employees, as is generally the case, this can nonetheless present a financial challenge to the firm, as it will be necessary to purchase and find an internal buyer for those shares at least once in every generation. It is for this reason that indirect ownership of a firm through a trust with a controlling stake, secured by a strong asset lock, offers a more effective way of ensuring continuing employee ownership.

Some recognition of the advantages of employee ownership has followed the publication of *Sharing Success: The Nuttall Review of Employee Ownership*.[12] The draft Finance Bill 2014 incorporates taxation relief measures on capital gains tax and inheritance tax associated with the transfer of business assets to encourage the formation of indirect employee ownership structures. These measures are intended to encourage existing owners or shareholders of incorporated businesses – sole traders and unlimited liability partnerships are excluded – to transfer some of their ownership to an employee ownership trust (EOT). There are also to be tax reliefs on bonus payments for employees of companies owned by an EOT. Such benefits apply only where there is a genuine transfer of control, so that the trust has more than 50 per cent of the company's ordinary share capital and carries more than 50 per cent both of voting powers and of rights to profit, and operates for the benefit of all employees.

It is doubtful whether these incentives will prove sufficiently attractive to counteract the appeal of other forms of asset transfer. The sale of the business to another company may be financially more advantageous for owners. As a consequence of the dominance of Corporation Ltd thinking, few owners, managers, policy makers and advisors have adequate knowledge of EOTs, or relevant expertise to facilitate their formation. This may be changing slowly as a consequence of the interest taken in them by the current Liberal-Democrat element in the coalition – notably Nick Clegg, the deputy prime minister, and Vince Cable, secretary of state for business, education and skills. This element of government policy is regrettably barely visible. As is noted in *Sharing Success*, the Employee Ownership Association and a number of other lobbying and transitioning organisations provide valuable information and guidance on employee ownership. But the review goes on to observe that their meagre resources are not enough if employee ownership is to enter the mainstream of the British economy. Much greater education, research, publicity and finance is needed.

Public Sector Mutualisation

Sharing Success also points to the programme of public sector mutualisation as an example of how employees can become owners of previously publicly owned assets, thereby offering an alternative to the Corporation Ltd and nationalised industry models that have historically dominated the private and public sectors.

Spinning out public services to a community interest company or a social enterprise entails significant costs, including planning, legal establishment and IT expenses. Some financial and business support has been made available in the United Kingdom through the Mutual Support Programme or Social Enterprise Investment Fund (SEIF). But such funds are only available for limited periods of time, and securing funding is a competitive and often lengthy process. Significant amounts of capital are often required to underwrite the complex liabilities that public-sector organisations transfer to spin-outs, whereas access to such capital is limited to all but the largest organisations.

Emerging financial markets, such as the social investment market, do not yet provide the levels of capitalisation required by social enterprises and mutuals. This is partly because of the limited capacity of the social investment market at the present time, as well as the risk that many fund managers perceive in financing organisations that may rely for the vast majority of their income on a few time-limited contracts. This is an area that is not helped by the lack of contract guarantees that many new service spin-outs have to deal with.[13]

There is also a danger that mutualisation will participate in its own discrediting and destruction if it provides a thinly disguised means of marketising public state provision. This may serve to expand the space Corporation Ltd can enter, as small mutuals struggle to compete with better resourced corporates. The current UK coalition government has shown no enthusiasm for the mutualisation of private-sector providers of public services. If there was real conviction that mutuals are unequivo-cally beneficial, then it would be expected that advocates of mutualisation would have no hesitation in guaranteeing a ballot to determine whether a particular organisation will be spun out of the private sector too.

Unless the mutualisation incorporates a diversity of stakeholders, however, it can amount to privatisation by employees through a disin-genuous process in which the relationship between the citizen and accountability for the provision of public goods and services is compro-mised and even severed. Where the mutualisation of public sector assets succeeds, there is also the risk that its expansion may enrich employees but without necessarily improving services for the wider community. Unless such mutualisation is adequately supported with relevant expertise and guarantees, its prospective members face considerable risk and uncertainty. Most obviously, mutualisation may be accompanied by the loss of comparatively generous public sector pensions.[14]

Mutuals may also risk being put out of business by bigger, better capitalised private competitors. In order to compete in a market defined by Corporation Ltd, members' terms and conditions may be degraded. Newly created mutuals are at a significant disadvantage as they are unlikely to possess the relevant in-house expertise on marketing, IT and human resources that is required to plan and operate successfully against private sector providers that have the advantage of economies of scale and business experience.

At risk in this contest is the ethos of public service as well as conti-nuity of the quality of the services provided. The mutualisation of slices of the public provision may also result in greater fragmentation of services, increased administration required to coordinate their efforts, and increasing cost pressures. Unless the playing field is levelled and assets are securely locked in, other providers, with greater reserves, who can temporarily undercut competitors and put them out of business will be the long-term winners. Such levelling is possible, as more encouraging experience from other European countries testifies:

> Where we see public service mutuals operating elsewhere in Europe at scale as mature parts of the public service economy, local and national policymakers have gone further than the UK in promoting the conditions for success, such as highly accessible business support, a focus on value-creation through participative governance and co-production and long-term commissioning strategies.[15]

An appropriate strategic response to the present scenario is to create the incentives and forms of support necessary to enable mutuals to compete and flourish. To this end, there should be an equivalent emphasis upon providing relevant support, participative governance and long-term commissioning, as well as equivalent facilitation of the mutualisation of private-sector providers. In all mutuals, assets must be securely locked, and surpluses must be ploughed back into improving their operation, or be more widely dispensed for benefit of the wider community.

Ownership and governance structures should not be restricted to employees, but should recognise and incorporate the contribution of diverse stakeholders to the effective and continuing operation of a mutual, perhaps using a two-tier supervisory board structure. Only then is it more likely that mutualisation will be supported by users and welcomed by employees. Up till now when employees have been balloted they have often declined the opportunity to form an EOT, as in West Essex and Shropshire Primary Care Trusts. Elsewhere, as in Medway and Kingston, the absence of such a ballot has been in defiance of demands by staff representatives who wished to put the option of mutualisation to the vote of their members.[16] Blocking such an option is clearly in contradiction to the democratic and collective values of mutuality. Such impositions give pause for reflection on the motivation of those who demand or endorse any such imposition.

Mutualisation offers a promising alternative to Corporation Ltd. It is more congruent with a modern democracy in which citizens/stakeholders take responsibility for the governance of corporations, and its closer integration of stakeholders with structures of ownership and governance is also more likely to foster ecological and social sustainability, as was argued in Chapter 13. Mutuality encourages greater engagement as well as less reckless stewardship of collectively created assets. It is also less socially divisive. as it inhibits differentials in income between an elite of wealthy shareholders and executives and a mass of other stakeholders. However it is imperfect, like all organisational forms, and subject to pathologies of passive ownership and weak governance. When it is adequately supported and safeguarded, though, mutualisation of public and private assets holds out the credible promise that abuses will be minimised, as stakeholders directly own and govern corporate assets, and so are best placed to ensure that they are carefully protected and sustained.

Conclusions

There are numerous alternative structures of ownership and governance to that of the typical PLC, including alternative corporations, and small local attempts to reimagine the economy. But these have been comparatively neglected and squeezed out by the dominance of the public limited company which we have characterised as Corporation Ltd. The importance of questions of governance and ownership mean that we have taken a close interest in EOTs, as these provide a radical alternative, with regard to governance as well as ownership, to Corporation Ltd.

Corporations accept few responsibilities, and enjoy limited liabilities, unlike human beings. The indifference and destructiveness of Corporation Ltd invites condemnation of its central role in the abuses of predatory capitalism. But it also demands the replacement of Corporation Ltd with alternative, socially and publicly accountable corporate forms of ownership and governance. This is precisely why we need to expose corporate abuses and challenge predatory forms of capitalism, but also to create and promote better regulated and less pathological ways of harnessing the constructive power of collective forms of organisation.

Notes and additional references

Notes

Chapter 1

1   European Commission, 'Tackling tax fraud and evasion in the EU – frequently asked questions', 2012, www.europa.eu/

2   Internal Revenue Service (IRS) press release, 'New tax gap estimates; compliance rates remain statistically unchanged from previous study', 6 January 2012, www.irs.gov/uac/irs (accessed 5 July 2013).

3   UK House of Commons Public Accounts Committee (HC PAC), *Tax Avoidance: Tackling Marketed Avoidance Schemes*, 29th Report, 19 February 2013, www.publications.parliament.uk/

4   HC PAC, *Tax Avoidance: The Role of Large Accountancy Firms*, 44th Report, 15 April 2013, www.publications.parliament.uk/

5   Action-Aid, 'Time to clean up: How Barclays promotes the use of tax havens in Africa', 2013, www.actionaid.org.uk

6   US Senate Joint Committee on Taxation, *Report of the Investigation of Enron Corporation and Related Entities regarding Federal Tax and Compensation Issues, and Policy Recommendations*, Washington DC: USGPO, 2003; US Bankruptcy Court Southern District of New York, *Third and Final Report of the Insolvency Examiner: In re WORLDCOM, INC., et al.*, Chapter 11, Case No. 02-13533 AJG, 2004. http://fl1.findlaw.com/news.findlaw.com/wsj/docs/worldcom/bkrexm12604rpt.pdf

7   *China Daily*, 25 November 2004, www.chinadaily.com.cn/ (accessed 4 January 2014).

8   Ibid.

9   A. Salz and R. Collins, *Salz Review: An Independent Review of Barclays' Business Practices*, London: Barclays Bank, 2013.

10   *Guardian*, 'George Osborne drafts new law on corporate tax dodgers', 28 February 2012, www.theguardian.com/business/2012/feb/28/

11   HM Treasury press release, 'Government action halts banking tax avoidance schemes', 27 February 2012, www.gov.uk/government/news/

12   Baker Tilly, 'International transfer pricing', www.bakertillyinternational.com/

13   Although the United Nations and more recently the OECD prefer to call them transnational corporations (TNCs), they will be referred to here in the more usual terminology as multinationals.

14   Unite the Union and War on Want, *Change to Win: Alliance Boots & the Tax Gap*, 2013, www.unitetheunion.org/uploaded/documents/

15 R. H. Coase, *The Nature of the Firm*, 1937, reprinted in *The Firm, the Market and the Law*, Chicago, Ill.: University of Chicago Press, 1988.

16 Action-Aid, 'Addicted to tax havens: The secret life of the FTSE 100', 2011, www.actionaid.org.uk/sites/default/files/doc_lib/addicted_to_tax_ havens.pdf (accessed 25 April 2014).

17 For more detailed treatment see Sol Picciotto, *International Business Taxation: A Study in the Internationalization of Business Regulations*, 1992, www.taxjustice.net/cms/upload/pdf/ and Sol Picciotto, 'Is the international tax system fit for purpose, especially for developing countries?', International Centre for Tax and Development Working Paper 13, 2013, http://www.ictd.ac/

18 United Nations Conference on Trade and Development (UNCTAD), 'Tax incentives and foreign direct investment: a global survey', ASIT Advisory Studies No. 16, 2000, New York and Geneva: UNCTAD.

19 R. S. Avi-Yonah, 'Globalization and tax competition: implications for developing countries', Inter-American Development Bank, February 2001, publications.iadb.org/

20 The US IRS attempted to deal with the problem by treating such affiliates as 'contract manufacturers' under transfer pricing rules, but this approach proved hard to sustain.

21 J. Drucker, 'Google 2.4% rate shows how $60 billion lost to tax loopholes', Bloomberg, 21 October 2010, www.bloomberg.com/news; John Sandell, 'The double Irish and the Dutch sandwich: how some US companies are flummoxing the tax code', *Tax Notes International*, 2012, Vol. 67, No. 9, pp. 867–8; Tom Bergin 'Special report: how big tech stays offline on tax', Reuters, 23 July 2013; HC PAC, 'Tax avoidance – Google', 9th Report, 2013–14, p. 112.

22 E. Kleinbard, 'Stateless income', *Florida Tax Review*, 2011, No. 9, pp. 700–73.

Chapter 2

1 UK Department of Trade and Industry (DTI), *Guinness PLC*, London: The Stationery Office, 1997, p. 309.

2 H. Davies, *The Financial Crisis: Who is to Blame?* Cambridge: Polity, 2010, p. 11.

3 *Guardian*, 'Bank of America's Countrywide found guilty of mortgage fraud', 23 October 2013, www.theguardian.com/

4 Financial Conduct Authority (FCA) press release, 'FCA fines Lloyds Banking Group firms a total of £28,038,800 for serious sales incentive failings', 11 December 2013, www.fca.org.uk/news/press-releases/

5 European Commission press release, 'Commission fines banks €1.71 billion for participating in cartels in the interest rate derivatives

industry', 4 December 2013, http://europa.eu/rapid/press-release_IP-13-1208_en.htm?locale=en (accessed 25 April 2014).

6 US Senate Permanent Subcommittee on Investigations, *US Vulnerabilities to Money Laundering, Drugs, and Terrorist Financing: HSBC Case History*, Washington DC, 2012.

7 BBC News, 'Standard Chartered hit by $300m in Iran fines', 10 December 2012, www.bbc.co.uk/news/business-20669650 (accessed 25 April 2014).

8 US Department of Financial Services press release, 'Cuomo administration reaches reform agreement with Deloitte over Standard Chartered consulting flaws', 18 June 2013, www.dfs.ny.gov/about/press2013/pr1306181.htm (accessed 25 April 2014).

9 UK DTI, *Mirror Group Newspapers plc*, London: The Stationery Office, 2001, p. 367.

10 P. Sikka, 'Audit policy-making in the UK: the case of the auditor's considerations in respect of going concern', *European Accounting Review*, 1992, Vol. 1, No. 2, pp. 349–92; P. Sikka, 'The politics of restructuring the standard setting bodies: the case of the UK's Auditing Practices Board', *Accounting Forum*, 2002, Vol. 26, No. 2, pp. 97–125.

11 After the biggest banking fraud of the 20th century at the Bank of Credit and Commerce International (BCCI), the UK government imposed a duty on financial sector auditors to report fraud to the regulators. However, there is no 'duty' to detect fraud even though accounting firms routinely sell such services under the rubric of 'forensic accounting', for extra fees. See P. Sikka, A. Puxty, H. Willmott and C. Cooper, 'The impossibility of eliminating the expectations gap: some theory and evidence', *Critical Perspectives on Accounting*, 1998, Vol. 9, No. 3, pp. 299–330.

12 [2007] EWCA Civ 910; [1990] 1 All ER HL 568.

13 *Caparo Industries plc v Dickman & Others* [1990] 1 All ER HL 568.

14 M. Mayer, *The Greatest-Ever Bank Robbery: The Collapse of the Savings and Loan Industry*, New York: Scribner, 1992.

15 N. Leeson and E. Whitley, *Rogue Trader*, London: Little, Brown, 1996.

16 US Senate Committee on Foreign Relations, *The BCCI Affair (A Report by Senator John Kerry and Senator Hank Brown)*, Washington DC: USGPO, 1992, p. 276.

17 After the Enron and WorldCom frauds Andersen was dissolved.

18 *Independent*, 'Alistair Darling: We were two hours from the cashpoints running dry', 18 March 2011, www.independent.co.uk/news/people/profiles/

19 The IASB is a private sector body primarily funded and populated by major corporations and the big four accounting firms. It also receives some money from the European Union, and since 2005 all EU listed companies are required to comply with IFRSs. The IASB is owned by the IFRS Foundation (previously known as the IASC Foundation) and is registered in the tax haven of Delaware.

20 *Financial Times*, 'US banks fear being forced to take $5,000bn back on balance sheets', 4 June 2008, www.ft.com/cms/

21 N. Hildyard, *A (Crumbling) Wall of Money Financial Bricolage, Derivatives and Power*, London: Cornerhouse, 2008, p. 30, www.thecornerhouse. org.uk

22 US Bankruptcy Court Southern District of New York, *In re Lehman Brothers Holding Inc., Report of Anton R. Valukas, 11 March 2010*, p. 735, http:// jenner.com/lehman/VOLUME%203.pdf

23 Ibid., p. 750.

24 *Accountancy Age*, 'E&Y sued over Lehmans audit', 21 December 2010, www.accountancyage.com

25 Reuters, 30 October 2008, www.reuters.com/article/ (accessed 18 January 2014).

26 BBC News, 'Credit crunch at $1.2 trillion', 25 March 2008, http://news. bbc.co.uk/1/hi/business/7313637.stm (accessed 25 April 2014).

27 P. Sikka, 'Financial crisis and the silence of the auditors', *Accounting, Organizations and Society*, 2009, Vol. 34, Nos. 6/7, pp. 868–73.

28 US Bankruptcy Court for the District of Delaware, *Final Report of Michael J. Missal Bankruptcy Court Examiner: In re New Century Trs. Holdings, Inc. a Delaware corporation, et al.*, 29 February 2008, p. 9, graphics8.nytimes. com/packages/pdf/business/Final_Report_New_Century.pdf

29 *Japan Times*, 'CPAs in Kanebo fraud avoid prison', 10 August 2006, www. japantimes.co.jp/news/

30 BBC News, 'Ex-Kanebo bosses in fraud arrest', 29 July 2005, http://news. bbc.co.uk/

31 *Accountancy Age*, 'Misuzu operations formally halt in Japan' 1 August 2007, http://www.accountancyage.com

32 US Senate Permanent Subcommittee on Investigations, *US Tax Shelter Industry: The Role of Accountants, Lawyers and Financial Professionals – Four KPMG Case Studies: FLIP, OPIS, BLIS and SC2*, Washington DC: US Senate, pp. 4 and 8.

33 US IRS press release, 'KPMG to Pay $456 million for criminal violations', 29 August 2005, www.irs.gov/uac

34 US Attorney for the Southern District of New York, press release, 'Manhattan U.S. attorney announces agreement with Ernst & Young LLP to pay $123 million to resolve federal tax shelter fraud investigation', 1 March 2013, www.justice.gov/usao/nys/

Chapter 3

1 *Salomon v. Salomon & Co Ltd* [1897] A.C. 22.

2 UK House of Commons Treasury Select Committee, 5th Report HC, 24 April 2008.

3   UK Parliamentary Commission on Banking Standards, April 2013, www. parliament.uk/

4   D. McBarnet and P. Schmidt, 'Corporate accountability through creative enforcement: human rights, the Alien Tort Claims Act and the limits of legal impunity', in D. McBarnet and A. Voiculescu (eds), *The New Corporate Accountability*, Cambridge: Cambridge University Press, 2007, pp. 148–76.

5   *Kiobel v. Royal Dutch Petroleum Co.*, US Supreme Court, 133 Supreme Court 1659, 2013.

Chapter 4

1   For a general account of the takeover and its consequences see M. Bose, *Manchester Disunited: Trouble and Takeover at the World's Richest Football Club*, London: Aurum Press, 2007.

2   Companies Act 2006, ss. 677–82. There are detailed exceptions in respect of private companies which might be relied on by persons in receipt of assistance after the shares have been purchased by loans from other sources.

3   UK Department for Business, Innovation and Skills, *Report on the Affairs of Phoenix Venture Holdings Limited, MG Rover Group Limited and 33 Other Companies*, 2009, www.insolvencydirect.bis.gov.uk

4   UK National Audit Office, *The Intercity East Coast Passenger Rail Franchise*, HC 824 Session 2010–11, 24 March 2011, London: The Stationery Office, www.nao.org.uk/

5   A similar proposal was put to a referendum in Switzerland in mid-2013 but failed to secure the necessary majority.

Chapter 5

1   J. Beatty, *The World According to Drucker*, New York: Orion, 1998, p. 82.

2   B. S. Frey, *Not Just for the Money: An Economic Theory of Personal Motivation*, Cheltenham: Edward Elgar, 1997, p. 20.

3   Ibid., p. 24. The reference is to F. Hirsch, *The Social Limits to Growth*, Cambridge, Mass.: Harvard University Press, 1976, p. 143.

4   A. Smith, *An Inquiry into the Nature and Causes of the Wealth of Nations*, Ch. 11, Part II (first published 1776), Oxford: Oxford University Press, 1993, p. 152.

5   A. Smith, *The Theory of Moral Sentiments*, Part VI, Section I, pp. 213–14 (first published 1759), New York: Dover, 2006.

6   US Congress, Dodd–Frank Wall Street Reform and Consumer Protection Act, 2010, Public Law 111-203.

7   A. Smith, *The Wealth of Nations*, p. 22.

8   M. Friedman, *Capitalism and Freedom*, Chicago, Ill.: Chicago University Press, 1962, p. 133.

9   A. A. Alchian and H. Demsetz, 'Production, information costs, and economic organisation', *American Economic Review*, 1972, Vol. 62, p. 778.

10   M. C. Jensen and W. H. Meckling, 'Theory of the firm: managerial behaviour, agency costs and ownership structure', *Journal of Financial Economics*, 1976, Vol. 3, pp. 305–60.

11   E. Sternberg, *Corporate Governance: Accountability in the Marketplace*, London: Institute of Economic Affairs, 2004, p. 37.

12   L. L. Lan and L. Heracleous, 'Rethinking agency theory: the view from law', *Academy of Management Review*, 2010, Vol. 35, No. 2, pp. 294–314.

Chapter 6

1   T. Levitt, 'The dangers of social responsibility', *Harvard Business Review*, 1958.

2   A. Chandler, *The Visible Hand: The Managerial Revolution in American Business*, Cambridge Mass: Beknap Press of Harvard University, 1977, p. 1.

3   M. Friedman, *Capitalism and Freedom*, Chicago, Ill.: Chicago University Press, 1962.

4   R. Khurana, *From Higher Aims to Hired Hands*, Princeton, N.J.: Princeton University Press, 2007.

5   UK Committee on the Financial Aspects of Corporate Governance: *The Cadbury Report*, December 1992, www.jbs.cam.ac.uk/cadbury/report/ (accessed 25 April 2014).

6   M. Heffernan, *Wilful Blindness*, London: Simon & Schuster, 2011, p. 214.

7   Ibid., p. 222.

8   See http://blog.lookuppage.com/2010/05/case-study-bp-oil-spill-.html (accessed 25 April 2014).

9   See http://www.bp.com/en/global/corporate/sustainability.html (accessed 25 April 2014).

10   See http://www.benjerry.co.uk

Chapter 7

1   P. Augar, *The Death of Gentlemanly Capitalism: The Rise and Fall of London's Investment Banks*, London: Penguin, 2008.

2   G. K. Ingham, *Capitalism Divided? The City and Industry in British Social Development*, Cambridge: Polity Press, 1984.

3   M. Moran, *The Politics of the Financial Services Revolution: the USA, UK, and Japan*, Basingstoke: Macmillan, 1991; M. Moran, *The British Regulatory State: High Modernism and Hyper-Innovation*, Oxford: Oxford University Press, 2003.

4   Philip Augar, *The Greed Merchants*, London: Penguin, 2006; Philip Augar, *Chasing Alpha*, London: Random House, 2009.

5   See the discussions in M. Lounsbury and P. M. Hirsch, 'Markets on trial: toward a policy-oriented economic sociology', in M. Lounsbury and P. M. Hirsch (eds), *Research in the Sociology of Organizations*, Bingley, UK: Emerald, 2010.

6   For details of these markets and their contribution to the financial crisis see G. Morgan, 'Legitimacy in financial markets: credit default swaps in the current crisis', *Socio-Economic Review*, 2010, Vol. 8, No. 1, pp. 17–45; G. Morgan, 'Market formation and governance in international financial markets: the case of OTC derivatives', *Human Relations*, 2008, Vol. 61, No. 5, pp. 637–60.

7   Nassim Nicholas Taleb, *The Black Swan*, London: Penguin, 2008.

8   Robert Peston, *How Do We Fix This Mess?* London: Hachette, 2012.

9   For details of the AIG debacle see Roddy Boyd, *Fatal Risk*, New York: John Wiley, 2011.

10 Andrew Ross Sorkin, *Too Big to Fail*, London: Penguin, 2010.

11 Ewald Engelen et al., 'Reconceptualizing financial innovation: frame, conjuncture and bricolage', *Economy and Society*, 2010, Vol. 39, No. 1, pp. 33–63; Ewald Engelen et al., *After the Great Complacence: Financial Crisis and the Politics of Reform*, Oxford: Oxford University Press, 2011.

12 BBC News, 1 April 2014.

13 A. Brummer, *The Crunch: How Greed and Incompetence Sparked the Credit Crisis*, London: Random House, 2009.

14 Michael Lewis, *The Big Short*, London: Penguin, 2011.

15 J. Froud and K. Williams, 'Private equity and the culture of value extraction', *New Political Economy*, 2007, Vol. 12, No. 3; Julie Froud, Sarah Green and Karel Williams, 'Private equity and the concept of brittle trust', *Sociological Review*, 2012, Vol. 60, No. 1, pp. 1–24; P. Folkman et al., 'Private equity: levered on capital or labour?' *Journal of Industrial Relations*, 2009, Vol. 51, No. 4, pp. 517–27.

Chapter 8

1   *Hutton v. West Cork Railway Co.* (1883) 23 Chancery Division 654.

2   Limited liability was not made an automatic aspect of incorporation in Britain until 1856 but is now regarded as an essential aspect of almost all forms of incorporated business enterprises.

3   A. Berle and G. Means, *The Modern Corporation and Private Property*, 1932, 2nd edn, Harcourt, Brace& World, 1967.

4   Department for Business, Innovation and Skills, *The Kay Review of UK Equity Markets and Long-Term Decision-Making: Final Report*, July 2012, www.bis.gov.uk/

5   Thorstein Veblen, *The Theory of Business Enterprise*, New York: Scribners

1912. Other classic accounts of the corporation as a social institution include P. Selznick, *TVA and the Grass Roots: A Study in the Sociology of Formal Organization*, Berkeley, Calif.: University of California Press, 1949, and A. Gouldner, *Patterns of Industrial Bureaucracy*, New York: Free Press, 1964. For a more recent contributions see J. Bakan, *The Corporation: The Pathological Pursuit of Profit and Power*, New York: Free Press, 2004.

6   T. Piketty, *Capitalism in the Twenty-First Century*, Cambridge Mass.: Harvard University Press, 2014.

Chapter 9

1   T. Hadden, *The Control of Corporate Groups*, London: Institute of Advanced Legal Studies, 1983.
2   For a comparative account of structures in different jurisdictions see T. Hadden, 'Regulating corporate groups: an international perspective', in J. McCahery, S. Picciotto and C. Scott (eds), *Corporate Control and Accountability*, Oxford: Clarendon Press, 1993, pp. 343–70.
3   International Financial Reporting Standard 8; see further T. Hadden, 'Accountable governance in corporate groups: the interrelationship of law and accounting', *Australian Accounting Review*, 2012, Vol. 22, No. 2, pp. 117–28 (see p. 121). The way in which these standards are drawn up is discussed in Chapter 2.
4   Financial and Accounting Standards Board, Interpretation 48 on Accounting for Uncertainty in Income Tax, 2006, www.fasb.org/cs/
5   Office of the United Nations High Commissioner for Human Rights, *Guiding Principles on Business and Human Rights: Implementing the United Nations 'Protect, Respect and Remedy'*, Human Rights Council Resolution 17/4, 16 June 2011.
6   T. Hadden, 'Accountable governance in corporate groups', p. 117.
7   F. Clarke and G. Dean, *Indecent Disclosure: Gilding the Corporate Lily*, Cambridge: Cambridge University Press, 2007, ch. 9.
8   Introduced under regulatory approval by the Australian Securities and Investment Commission; for a detailed account of its use see Clarke and Dean, *Indecent Disclosure*, pp. 161 ff.
9   For a general account see V. Emmerich and J. Sonnenschein, *Konzernrecht*, Munich, Germany: C. H. Beck, 1989.
10   For a more detailed account see S. Picciotto, *Regulating Global Corporate Capitalism*, Cambridge: Cambridge University Press, 2011, ch. 5.

Chapter 10

1   Oxfam's report, *Tax Havens: Releasing the Hidden Billions for Poverty Eradication*, 2000 was very influential in bringing out these issues; see also academic work such as D. Bräutigam, O.-H. Fjeldstad and M. Moore

(eds), *Taxation and State Building in Developing Countries: Capacity and Consent*, Cambridge: Cambridge University Press, 2008.

2   US Government Accountability Office, *Company Formations: Minimal Ownership Information is Collected and Available*, Doc. no. GAO-06-376, Washington DC, 2006.

3   J. C. Sharman 'Shopping for anonymous shell companies: an audit study of anonymity and crime in the international financial system', *Journal of Economic Perspectives*, 2010, Vol. 24, No. 4, pp. 127–40; M. Findley, D. Nielson and J. C. Sharman, 'Global shell games: testing money launderers' and terrorist financiers' access to shell companies', 2013, www.griffith.edu.au/business-government/

4   Council Directive 2003/48/EC on taxation of savings income in the form of interest payments. Austria, Belgium and Luxembourg were allowed to apply a withholding tax, the proceeds of which are handed over to the country of destination, because they refused to lift bank secrecy until non-EU states agreed to do so. Negotiations with such states, especially Switzerland and other tax havens such as Liechtenstein and the Channel Islands, have been pursued every since. Proposals for improvement of this Directive have been under consideration since 2008. In the meantime, this has been overtaken by the introduction of FATCA and the move towards a global system for automatic exchange of information.

5   G8, Lough Erne Leaders' Communiqué, 2013, https://www.gov.uk/government/

6   R. Murphy, 'Country-by-country reporting. accounting for globalisation locally', Tax Justice Network, 2012, www.taxresearch.org.uk/Documents/CBC2012.pdf (accessed 25 April 2014).

7   See www.publishwhatyoupay.org/

8   The EITI Principles were agreed at a conference in London in 2003, and the EITI Standard, extending to implementation, governance and management, was adopted in 2013: see http://eiti.org/.

9   Wall Street Reform and Consumer Protection Act 2010, s.1504. However, the oil lobby has been using legal pressures and other tactics to hinder the drafting of the detailed regulations by the SEC.

10   Directive 2013/34/EU, to be implemented by member states within two years.

11   For a more detailed and technical discussion see S. Picciotto, 'Can the OECD mend the international tax system?' *Tax Notes International*, 2013, Vol. 71, No. 2, pp. 1105–15.

12   S. Picciotto, 'Is the international tax system fit for purpose, especially for developing countries?' ICTD Working Paper 13, 2013.

13   See the series of articles by Michael Durst in *Tax Management Transfer Pricing Reports* in 2013 and 2014, available at http://www.ictd.ac/en/publications-unitary-taxation (accessed 25 April 2014).

14   The European Union has no competence for direct taxation, so the proposal was put forward as a measure to enhance the internal market

by facilitating capital movements. Being a fiscal measure it cannot be approved by the ordinary procedure of weighted majority voting, but requires unanimity. However, it may be possible to use the 'enhanced cooperation procedure' which provides for adoption of measures by at least nine states, binding only on them (see Treaty on European Union article 20), as has been done for the financial transactions tax. Algirdas Šemeta, the EU Commissioner responsible for taxation, has recently stressed the relevance of the CCCTB for 'the wider work against corporate tax avoidance' as well as for simplifying cross-border business, and has urged stronger political support (in a speech to an ECON Committee meeting in Brussels, 26 November 2013).

15 The objection made is that national governments would lose sovereignty by giving up the power to define the corporate tax base. However, the CCCTB would only apply to companies with cross-border activities, and governments generally use their power to define the tax base to compete with each other in offering tax breaks to attract investment.

16 See R. Murphy and P. Sikka, *Unitary Taxation: Tax Base and the Role of Accounting*, International Centre for Tax and Development, forthcoming 2014.

17 OECD, *Revised Discussion Draft on Transfer Pricing Aspects of Intangibles*, 2013, Paris: OECD, para 164, p. 40.

18 See the sections by India and China in Chapter 10 of the *UN Practical Manual on Transfer Pricing* (2013); the reference to a global formulary approach is in section 10.2.6.3 by China. The preference of India's then competent authority, Sanjay Mishra, for profit-split was revealed by his US counterpart Michael Danilack in forthright remarks at a practitioner meeting in January 2013; see K. A. Parillo and S. Trivedi, 'U.S. competent authority has harsh words about India', *Worldwide Tax Daily*, 4 February 2013. Mishra's subsequent removal was not unconnected to US complaints.

19 See US Treasury Notice 94-40 (1994 IRB LEXIS 213), which states that the main apportionment factor should be the traders' remuneration.

20 M. Durst, 'Analysis of a formulary system, Part VI: Building the formula', *Tax Management Transfer Pricing Reports*, Vol. 22, No. 18) 23 Jan. 2014, also available from www.ictd.ac/en/publications-unitary-taxation

21 M. A. Sullivan, 'With billions at stake, Glaxo puts U.S. APA program on trial', *Tax Notes International*, 2013, Vol. 34, pp. 456–63. Ironically, Glaxo made the opposite argument when the Canadian authorities challenged the pricing of the Zantac licences to Glaxo Canada, on the grounds that they could be acquired for less under compulsory licences from generic producers. Glaxo argued that such prices were not comparable to what it offered in the comprehensive licence package, which included the brand name.

22 Evaluations of these proposals will be made by the BEPS Monitoring Group, a network of international tax specialists sponsored

and supported by the main tax justice organisations, and published at http://bepsmonitoringgroup.wordpress.com/
23 See OECD, *Addressing Base Erosion and Profit Shifting*, 2013, Paris: OECD, and sources cited in ch. 2.
24 J. J. Henry, *The Price of Offshore Revisited*, 2013, www.taxjustice.net/

Chapter 11

1 J. Fox and J. W. Lorsch, 'What good are shareholders?' *Harvard Business Review*, 2012, Vol. 90, Nos. 7/8, pp. 48–57.
2 *Economist*, 'The endangered public company: the rise and fall of a great invention, and why it matters', 19 May 2012.
3 G. Kirkpatrick, 'The corporate governance lessons from the financial crisis', *Financial Market Trends*, 2009, Paris: OECD, p. 96.
4 House of Commons Treasury Committee, *Banking Crisis: Reforming Corporate Governance and Pay in the City*, London: The Stationery Office, 2009, quoted in M. Arden, 'Regulating the conduct of directors', *Journal of Corporate Law Studies*, 2010, No. 10.
5 FSA, *The Turner Review: A Regulatory Response To The Global Banking Crisis*, 2009, London: FSA, para. 2.8. Available at: www.fsa.gov.uk/pubs/other/turner_review.pdf (accessed 25 April 2014).
6 HM Treasury, *A Review of Corporate Governance in UK Banks and Other Financial Industry Entities*, 2009, http://webarchive.nationalarchives.gov.uk/+/http:/www.hm-treasury.gov.uk/d/walker_review_261109.pdf (accessed 25 April 2014). See p. 9 (Executive Summary): 'One of the problems that exist is the fact that little is known about the characteristics of boards of banks'; D. Ferreira, T. Kirchmaier and D. Metzger, 'Boards of banks', ECGI Finance Working Paper No. 289/2010, http://ssrn.com/abstract=1620551 (accessed 25 April 2014).
7 L. M. Friedman, *A History of American Law*, New York: Simon & Schuster Touchstone, 1973, p.168.
8 P. Maier, 'The revolutionary origins of the American corporation', *William and Mary Quarterly*, 1993, 3rd Ser., pp. 51–84.
9 C. A. Dunleavy, 'Corporate governance in late 19th century Europe and the United States: the case of shareholder voting rights', in K. Hopt et al. (eds), *Comparative Corporate Governance*, Oxford: Oxford University Press, 1998, p. 15.
10 L. L. Lan and L. Heracleous, 'Rethinking agency theory', 2010, see Ch. 5 note 12.
11 Companies Act 2006, Part 10, Chapter 2, s. 170, Scope and nature of general duties.
12 Ibid., s. 172, Duty to promote the success of the company.
13 Ibid., s. 994, Petition against unfairly prejudicial conduct.

14 *Report of the Committee on the Financial Aspects of Corporate Governance*, London: Gee & Co., 1992.

15 J. Solomon, *Corporate Governance and Accountability*, 2nd edn., Chichester: John Wiley & Son, 2007, p. 188.

16 *Cadbury Report*, Section 6.1 Accountability of Boards to Shareholders.

17 Financial Reporting Council, first published July 2010, revised September 2012.

18 Reuters, 'Update 2 – U.S. probing high-speed trading, attorney general says', 4 April 2014. Available at: www.reuters.com/article/2014/04/04/congress-justice-highspeed-idUSL1N0MW0NA20140404 (accessed 5 May 2014).

19 K. Camfferman and S. A. Zeff, *Financial Reporting and Global Capital Markets: A History of the International Accounting Standards Committee, 1973–2000*, Oxford: Oxford University Press, 2007.

20 CNN Money, 'Accounting group sought Enron donation', 13 February 2002, http://money.cnn.com/2002/02/13/news/enron_volker/ (accessed 18 February 2013).

21 An attempt was made to achieve some of these objectives in the United States through the Corporate and Auditing Accountability and Responsibility Act of 2002, otherwise known as the Sarbanes–Oxley Act. It was prompted by the apparent growth of fraudulent accounting, and explicitly sought to limit the power of the 'big four' auditors. But the Act has apparently had little effect in this. Their monopolistic control of the market was emphasised by PwC's CEO stating, in effect, that if an audit certificate was really required to confirm the accounts as true and fair, then they would cost a whole lot more.

22 European Commission press release, 'Reform of the EU statutory audit market – frequently asked questions', 3 April 2014, http://europa.eu/rapid/press-release_MEMO-14-256_en.htm?locale=en (accessed 25 April 2014).

23 In April 2014, the European Parliament passed a resolution stating that companies listed in the European Union, credit institutions and insurance undertakings will be required to change their statutory auditors after a maximum engagement period of ten years. Member States can choose to extend the ten-year period up to ten additional years if tenders are carried out, and by up to 14 additional years in case of joint audit, i.e. if the audited company appoints more than one audit firm to carry out its audit. See European Commission press release, 'European Parliament backs Commission proposals on new rules to improve the quality of statutory audit', 3 April 2014; http://europa.eu/rapid/press-release_STATE MENT-14-104_en.htm (accessed 25 April 2014). The 10–24 year rule is a marked concession to lobbying by big firms.

24 Article 226 of the French Code des Sociétés Commerciales of 1996 provides for shareholders holding at least 10 per cent of the total shares

to petition the court for the appointment of experts to report on any specific matter. The power is broadly interpreted and widely used. See Dalloz, *Code des Sociétés* (annual editions) and M. Pariente, *Les Groupes de Sociétés*, Paris: Litec, 1992.

25 A. Sykes, 'Proposals for a reformed system of corporate governance to achieve internationally competitive long term performance', in N. Dimsdale and M. Prevezer, *Capital Markets and Corporate Governance*, Oxford: Clarendon Press, 1994, p. 111–12.

26 D. Zorn 'Here a chief, there a chief: the rise of the CFO in the American firm', *American Sociological Review*, 2004, Vol. 69, pp. 345–64.

27 Kommission zur Moderniesierung der Deutschen Unternehmensmitbestimmung, 2006, kohte.jura.uni-halle.de/

28 J. Solomon, *Corporate Governance and Accountability*, pp. 4–5.

29 Cmnd. 6706, HMSO, 1977.

30 Introductory paragraph of the Statute for a European Company, summary available online at http://europa.eu/legislation_summaries/ employment_and_social_policy/social_dialogue/l26016_en.htm

31 S. Ghoshal, 'Bad management theories are destroying good management practices', *Academy of Management Learning and Education*, 2006, Vol. 4, No. 1, p. 85.

32 Ibid., p. 75.

33 S. Murray, 'Short-term tone in traditional MBA teaching begins to fade', *Financial Times*, 8 July 2013.

Chapter 12

1 *Guardian*, 7 August 2009, www.theguardian.com/uk/business?/

2 For an excellent account of how this switch from financial to state crisis occurred see M. Blyth, *Austerity: The History of a Dangerous Idea*, Oxford: Oxford University Press, 2013.

3 *Guardian*, 13 December 2013.

4 Liikanen et al., *High-Level Expert Group on Reforming the Structure of the EU Banking Sector*, Brussels, 2 October 2012.

5 Independent Commission on Banking, *The Vickers Report*, 12 September 2011, http://webarchive.nationalarchives.gov.uk/ + /bankingcommission. independent.gov.uk (accessed 25 April 2014).

6 The *Wall Street Journal* reported on 14 January 2014 that regulators were softening their attitude on reserves. It stated that 'the announcement is the latest in a series of amendments to the aggressive new rules that regulators drew up in reaction to the 2008 financial crisis, in an effort to make the financial system safer … the industry has managed to persuade regulators that their plans were overzealous.'

7 E. Helleiner et al., 'Reforming the global financial architecture', *Socio-Economic Review*, 2011, Vol. 9, No. 3, pp. 567–96; G. Morgan, 'Reforming

OTC markets', *European Business Organization Law Review*, 2012, Vol. 13, No. 3, pp. 391–412.

8   *Financial Times*, 14 February 2014.

9   J. Froud et al., *Financialization and Strategy*, London: Routledge, 2006; W. Lazonick and M. O'Sullivan, 'Maximizing shareholder value: a new ideology for corporate governance', *Economy and Society*, 2000, Vol. 29, No. 1, pp. 13–35; L. A. Stout, *The Shareholder Value Myth: How Putting Shareholders First Harms Investors, Corporations, and the Public*, San Francisco, Calif.: Berrett-Koehler, 2012; G. F. Davis, *Managed by the Markets: How Finance Re-Shaped America*, Oxford: Oxford University Press, 2009.

10 C. Mayer, *Firm Commitment: Why the Corporation Is Failing Us and How to Restore Trust in It*, Oxford: Oxford University Press, 2013.

11 Department for Business, Innovation and Skills, *The Kay Review of UK Equity Markets and Long-Term Decision-Making: Final Report*, July 2012 www.bis.gov.uk/

Chapter 13

1   J. Bakan, *The Corporation: The Pathological Pursuit of Profit and Power*, New York: Free Press, 2004.

2   K. Polanyi, *The Great Transformation*, Boston, Mass.: Beacon Press, 2001.

3   E. F. Schumacher, *Small is Beautiful*, New York: Harper & Row, 1989.

4   I. Berlin, *Two Concepts of Liberty*, Oxford: Clarendon Press, 1969.

5   N. Georgescu-Roegen, *La Decroissance*, Paris: Sang de la Terre, 1995.

6   C. Williams, *A Commodified World? Mapping the Limits of Capitalism*, London: Zed, 2005.

7   J. K. Gibson-Graham, *The End of Capitalism (As We Knew It)*, Cambridge: Blackwell, 1996; and *A Postcapitalist Politics*, Minneapolis, Minn.: University of Minnesota Press, 2006.

8   P. North, *Local Money*, Dartington, UK: Green Books, 2010.

9   M. Parker, *Against Management*, Oxford: Polity, 2002; R. Locke, and J.-C. Spender, *Confronting Managerialism*, London: Zed, 2011; G. Pearson, *The Road to Co-operation*, Farnham: Gower, 2012.

10 D. Erdal, *Beyond the Corporation: Humanity Working*, London: Bodley Head, 2011; Ownership Commission, *Plurality, Stewardship and Engagement*, Borehamwood: Mutuo, 2012, http://ownershipcomm.org/files/

11 M. Albert, *Parecon: Life After Capitalism*, London: Verso, 2003.

12 Co-operatives UK, *The UK Co-operative Economy 2012: Alternatives to Austerity*, Manchester: Co-ops UK Ltd, 2012.

13   M. Maeckelbergh, *The Will of the Many: How the Alterglobalisation Movement is Changing the Face of Democracy*, London: Pluto, 2009.

14 M. Parker, V. Fournier and P. Reedy, *The Dictionary of Alternatives: Utopia and Organization*, Zed Books, 2007; M. Parker, V. Fournier, G. Cheney

and C. Land (eds), *The Companion to Alternatives*, London: Routledge, 2014.

Chapter 14

1   The Ownership Commission, *Plurality, Stewardship and Engagement*, Boreham Wood: Mutuo, 2012, p. 19; http://ownershipcomm.org/
2   M.-L. Djelic, 'When limited liability was (still) an issue: mobilization and politics of signification in 19th-century England', *Organization Studies*, 2013, Vol. 34, Nos 5–6, pp. 595–621.
3   W. Davies, *Reinventing the Firm*, London: Demos, 2009; www.demos.co.uk/files/
4   B. Paranque and H. C. Willmott, 'Cooperatives – saviours or gravediggers of capitalism? Critical performativity and the John Lewis Partnership', *Organization*, 2014 (in press).
5   S. Davies, 'Mutual benefit? A report for UNISON', London: UNISON, 2011, p. 24; see also C. Ham and P. Hunt, 'Membership governance in NHS trusts: a review for the Department of Health', University of Birmingham and Mutuo, 2008.
6   See www.socialenterprise.org.uk and Chapter 13.
7   P. Butler, 'Our mutual friends: better care or the end of the NHS', *Guardian*, 19 November 2010, www.guardian.co.uk/society/
8   R. Hazenberg, K. Hall and H. Ogden-Newton, *Public Service Mutuals: Spinning Out or Standing Still?* London: Royal Society of Arts, 2013, p. 22; www.thersa.org/
9   Private equity firms which now control around 15 per cent of employment, or 3 million employees in the UK private sector.
10 Kommission zur Modernisierung der deutschen Unternehmensmitbestimmung, 2006. The report was based only on the views of the so-called 'scientific' members since the representatives of employers and trade unions could not agree on whether to limit or extend the system.
11 Davies, *Reinventing the Firm*, p. 63; see also http://employeeownership.co.uk.
12 Employee Ownership Association, *Employee Ownership Impact Report: The Business Case for Employee Ownership*, March 2013 http://employee-ownership.co.uk/
13 Hazenberg et al., *Public Service Mutuals*, pp. 20–1.
14 Independent Public Service Pensions Commission, Final Report (the Hutton Report), March 2011, www.nhsbsa.nhs.uk/Documents/Pensions/hutton_final_100311.pdf (accessed 25 April 2014). Recommendation 16 declares that 'It is in principle undesirable for future non-public service workers to have access to public service pension schemes, given the increased long-term risk this places on the government and taxpayers'. If this view is adopted, then mutualisation will not be accompanied by the retention

of a public sector pension, unlike the example of Hull's City Health Care Partnership described earlier.

15   Hazenberg et al., *Public Service Mutuals*, p. 24; see also J. Bland, *Time to Get Serious: International Lessons for Developing Public Sector Mutuals*, Manchester: Co-operatives UK, 2011, www.uk.coop/

16   S. Davies, 'Mutual benefit?'

Additional References

Alexander, G. et al. (2012) *Exploring the Effectiveness of Public Service Mutuals in Comparison to In-House Provision*, Aspire Sussex, Cabinet Office, City Health Care Partnership CIC and University of Southampton, http://socialsciences. exeter.ac.uk/media/universityofexeter/collegeofsocialsciencesandinter nationalstudies/politics/projects/mme/Group_Project_Electronic_Copy.pdf (accessed 25 April 2014).

Grant Thornton (2013) 'Tax incentives for employee ownership', briefing paper, www.grant-thornton.co.uk

Mutuals Taskforce (2011) 'Out mutual friends: making the case for public service mutuals', London: Cabinet Office, http://mutuals.cabinetoffice.gov.uk/govern ment/ (accessed 25 April 2014).

Mutuals Taskforce (2012) 'Public service mutuals: the next steps', London: Cabinet Office, http://mutuals.cabinetoffice.gov.uk/documents/mutuals-task force-report-public-service-mutuals-next-steps (accessed 25 April 2014).

Oxera Consulting (2007) 'Oxera Tax-advantaged employee share schemes: analysis of productivity effects', report for HM Revenue & Customs, www. hmrc.gov.uk/research/tax-advantaged-overview.pdf (accessed 25 April 2014).

Postlethwaite, R. (2009) *Structuring Employee Ownership: A Guide to Trusts, Shares and Tax Help for Co-ownership*, London: Employee Ownership Association, March, http://employeeownership.co.uk/

Postlethwaite, R., Michie, J, Burns, P. and Nuttall, G. (2005) *Shared Company: How Employee Ownership Works*, London: Employee Ownership Association, www.employeeownership.co.uk/

The Corporate Reform Collective

The members of the Corporate Reform Collective who have compiled the book and drawn up the lengthy list of essential reforms to corporate law, accounting and audit rules, and international taxation are:

Tom Hadden: company lawyer and human rights actor from Northern Ireland and currently emeritus professor at Queens University Belfast. His most relevant publications are his seminal 1970s text *Company Law and Capitalism*, articles on corporate group structures in the 1980s and 1990s and most recently 'Accountable governance in corporate groups: the interrelationship of law and accounting' in the *Australian Accounting Review* (2012).

Paddy Ireland: company historian and development specialist and currently professor of law at the University of Bristol Law School, where he teaches corporate governance. He has written extensively on the history of company law and corporate theory. Selected publications include 'Limited liability, rights of control and the problem of corporate irresponsibility', *Cambridge Journal of Economics*, 2010; 'Corporate social responsibility in a neoliberal age' in P. Ytting and J. Marques, *Corporate Social Responsibility and Regulatory Governance*, 2009; and 'Financialization and corporate governance', *Northern Ireland Legal Quarterly*, 2009.

Glenn Morgan: professor of international management at Cardiff University and visiting professor at the Department of Business and Politics, Copenhagen Business School. His research interests lie in the changing nature of capitalism and the impact of globalisation and multinationals on national institutions, elites, regulation and the role of finance and financialisation. Recent edited books include *Capitalisms and Capitalism in the Twenty First century*, Oxford University Press, 2012, and *New Spirits of Capitalism: Crises, Justifications and Dynamics*, Oxford University Press, 2012.

Martin Parker: professor of organisation and culture at the School of Management, University of Leicester. His most relevant works are the authored *Against Management*, Polity, 2012, the co-authored *Dictionary of Alternatives: Utopianism and Organization*, Zed, 2007, and the co-edited *Companion to Alternative Organization*, Routledge, 2013.

Gordon Pearson: former company executive and current activist blogger on the impact of economic and behavioural theory on the practical realities of industrial management. His experience in mergers and acquisitions was the basis of his critique of accounting's short termism in *The Strategic Discount*. His critical books on theory and practice include *Strategic Thinking*, *The Competitive Organization*, *Integrity in Organizations*, *The Rise and Fall of Management* and *The Road to Co-operation*.

Sol Picciotto: international taxation expert and senior adviser to the Tax Justice Network, and currently emeritus professor of law at Lancaster University. His interests are international economic law, international business regulation, state theory and international capital, and law and social theory. His books include *International Business Taxation*, CUP, 1992; *Corporate Control and Accountability*, Clarendon, 1993; *Regulating International Business – Beyond Liberalization*, Macmillan, 1999; and *Regulating Global Corporate Capitalism*, CUP, 2011.

Prem Sikka: professor of accounting at the University of Essex. His research on accountancy, auditing, tax avoidance, tax havens, corporate governance, money laundering, insolvency and business affairs has been published in international scholarly journals, books, newspapers and magazines. He has appeared on radio and television programmes to comment on business matters, has advised and given evidence to parliamentary committees and is a regular contributor to the media. He has received the *Accountancy Exemplar* award from the American Accounting Association, the *Lifetime Achievement* award from the British Accounting and Finance Association and the *Working for Justice* award from the Tax Justice Network.

Hugh Willmott: author and activist on alternative forms of business structure, and currently research professor in organisational studies at Cardiff University. His research interests include organisation studies, managerial work, management education and learning, accounting in organisations and society, and social theory. His recent publications include *Introducing Organization Behaviour and Management*, Thomson, 2006; and *Oxford Handbook of Critical Management Studies*, Oxford University Press, 2011.

Index

Note: UK laws and bodies are listed alphabetically, those of other countries and international organisations under the country/organisation name. References to notes are in the format 194n11-21 for note 21 to chapter 11 on page 194.